The Cook Survives . . . is the ideal series of cookbooks for special occasions and particular situations. Designed by Pat McCormack to help you – the cook – enjoy yourself and keep on top of things in the kitchen, *The Cook Survives . . .* series offers useful hints for organizing your cooking, easy-to-cook, tasty menus and detailed recipes packed with helpful information.

The Cook Survives . . . Christmas and New Year will take the worry out of the festive season.

PAT McCORMACK

The Cook Survives . . .

Christmas and New Year

Illustrated by
Geraldine Foster

GRAFTON BOOKS
A Division of the Collins Publishing Group

LONDON GLASGOW
TORONTO SYDNEY AUCKLAND

Grafton Books
A Division of the Collins Publishing Group
8 Grafton Street, London W1X 3LA

Published by Grafton Books 1985

ISBN 0-586-06638-1

Printed and bound in Great Britain by
Cox & Wyman Ltd., Reading, Berks.

Set in Bembo

Contents

Introduction

Christmas seems to become more complicated by the year. What should be a relaxed and joyful holiday can leave 'the cook' so exhausted she sleeps through all the best bits!

The Cook Survives . . . offers menus that are very simple indeed but that rely heavily on the quality of the ingredients, so forget the Alka-Seltzer and the annual orgy of over-rich meal after meal and enjoy the true luxury of simply prepared good food with the bonus of lots more time to spend away from the kitchen relaxing.

HOW TO USE THE BOOK

The Cook Survives . . . gives menu suggestions day by day, but, of course, they can be swapped around. For instance, some people may prefer to have the traditional roast ribs of beef shown for New Year's Day on Christmas Day and vice versa. It is a good idea to look through each day's suggestions and decide what sort of meals will be most appropriate. Try to consider the holiday as a whole rather than a series of separate days. For instance, Boxing Day could become almost 'cook-free', even with a houseful! If you have the baked ham on Christmas Eve and roast turkey on Christmas Day, by adding a mixed salad, jacket potatoes, pickles and warm rolls to the two cold meats you have a lovely, simply prepared luncheon buffet.

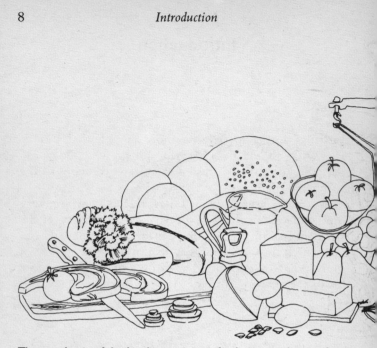

The emphasis of the book remains on fresh, top quality produce

For dinner choose something like the delicious beef in red wine with mushrooms which can be prepared in advance and frozen. All in all a very relaxed day for the cook!

Many recipes are suitable for freezing and clearly marked to that effect, but the emphasis of the book remains on fresh, top-quality produce.

Breakfasts are perhaps best left at fresh fruit juice and cereals or wholegrain toast, but a popular alternative is a full brunch at mid-morning and a good meal in the evening. Lists are invaluable at this time of year. Once you have decided on your menus it is easier to list everything needed in sections; then the non-perishables

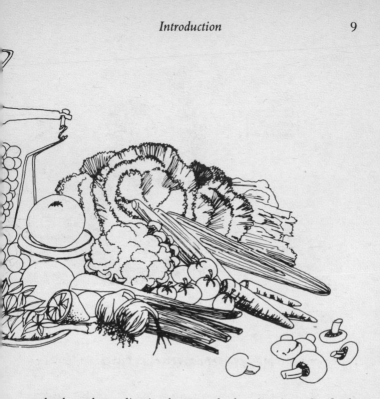

can be bought earlier in the month, leaving just the fresh essentials for last-minute shopping.

Innovations and improvements in transport mean that the traditional seasonal limits to what is on the market at Christmas-time no longer apply, and pretty well anything is available, at a price! New potatoes from Egypt, or strawberries flown in from Israel and California, although expensive, can be a particular delight in the midst of winter and well worth considering.

All main meals have time-tables and basic times for roasting are listed in the chart on page 53. Measures are given in both metric and imperial scales (don't mix the two) and no special equipment is needed.

Lists are invaluable at this time of the year

NOTE ON QUANTITIES

Most recipes show how many servings can be expected from the quantities given. The exceptions are the large birds, fish, or joints of meat where obviously many more could be served if necessary. The accompanying stuffing and sauce recipes are given in quantities to complement the particular joint or bird.

NB: ★ denotes recipes that are suitable for freezing.

On now to the all important question: 'What shall we have on . . .?'

New potatoes from Egypt or strawberries flown
from Israel and California . . .

Christmas Eve

Christmas Eve is always a busy day, with last-minute shopping, present-wrapping and cleaning on most cook's 'to do' lists, not to mention the fact that for many people it is also a working day! The tension can be disastrous and not the best start to a happy holiday. *The Cook Survives . . .* offers a relaxed start to the celebrations, whether dinner or a light supper is required. Our menus are easy, very tasty and light enough to be enjoyed even quite late at night. Working all day? Far too 'strung-up' to eat? Take half an hour off, pour a glass of wine, and relax – our Warming Light Supper will restore sanity and let you carry on with the final preparations with renewed 'gusto'!

MENU 1: Warming Light Supper

	page
Bean and Bacon Soup★	20
. . .	
Wholegrain Rolls★	21
. . .	
Small Mince Pies with Cinnamon Cream★	21

Kids want to go to bed at 4.00 p.m.? Don't give in! Try switching on *Disney Time* or more appropriately *Monster from the Deep* and serve our 'Sweet Dreams' Supper (fish is supposed to have *calming qualities*!).

Last minute present wrapping and cleaning

MENU 2: 'Sweet Dreams' Supper

	page
Old-fashioned Fish Pie★	23
. . .	
Tangerine Mousse★	24

Everything reasonably organized? Children a little older and what's needed is an enjoyable family meal to start the holiday in style? Why not try our very wholesome Family Dinner.

MENU 3: Family Dinner
(See Timetable page 42)

	page
Watercress Soup★ with Croutons	25

Fish is supposed to have calming qualities

. . .

. . .

Guests arriving and you want something a little more
sophisticated? The special 'Bombe' adds a festive touch.

MENU 4: Guest Dinner
(See Timetable page 43)

The office party goes on far too long and half the revellers come home with you!

MENU 5: 'Soak It Up' Supper

Out all day and need something that can be cooked automatically and served in seconds?

MENU 6: Automatic Supper

Just the two of you? Make the most of it with:

MENU 7: Romantic Candlelit Supper

Recipes

BEAN AND BACON SOUP*

Serves 6
   300g (12 oz) smoked streaky bacon, derinded and
     chopped
   50g (2 oz) celery
   200g (8 oz) onion   } finely chopped
   300g (12 oz) dried haricot beans, soaked overnight
   1.8 litres (3 pints) water
   3 stock cubes (chicken, lamb or vegetable)
   2 bay leaves
   4 cloves, whole
   freshly ground black pepper
   400g (1 lb) fresh tomatoes, skinned, seeded and chopped
   or
   397g (14 oz) tin of tomatoes, chopped
   salt

To Cook

1) Heat a large thick-based pan for a few moments then add the bacon pieces and cook in their own fat until browned. Spoon off any excess fat, leaving about 3 tablespoons in the pan.
2) Add the onions and celery and simmer gently until both are cooked and lightly coloured.
3) Put the soaked beans, water, stock cubes, bay leaves, cloves, pepper but *no* salt into the pan and simmer gently for 2 hours.
4) Stir in the tomatoes. Simmer again for 10 minutes. Check seasonings, adding salt now if required.

To Serve

The best way to serve a 'chunky' soup such as this, is to ladle it into soup plates from a tureen placed in the centre of the table. Almost any large bowl or casserole dish will double as a tureen and a brightly coloured tea cloth or napkin tied around the pot can look most appealing.

Warm wholemeal rolls and a good country butter are delicious as an accompaniment to this soup.

WHOLEGRAIN ROLLS*

Gives 16 rolls approx.
  15g (½ oz) salt
  750g (2 lb) granary bread flour
  15g (½ oz) lard
  25g (¾ oz) yeast (fresh or dried)
  450 ml (¾ pint) warm water

To Cook
1) Mix the salt into the flour in a large bowl. Rub in the lard with the fingertips.
2) Make a well in the centre of the mixture and add the yeast and enough of the warmed water to make a smooth dough. Knead for 5 minutes. Let stand in a warm place for 30 minutes.
3) Divide the dough into 50g (2 oz) pieces; form these into rolls and place on greased baking trays. Leave to rise in a warm place for 35 minutes then bake at 230°C (450°F) Gas Mark 8 for 10–20 minutes – 10 minutes for soft rolls; 15–20 for crisp rolls.

SMALL MINCE PIES* WITH CINNAMON CREAM

Gives 12 mince pies
  300g (12 oz) shortcrust pastry (see Basic Preparations, page 151)

For the Mincemeat
  300g (12 oz) apples, peeled, cored and chopped
  75g (3 oz) soft brown sugar
  50g (2 oz) sultanas
  50g (2 oz) seedless raisins
  50g (2 oz) currants
  50g (2 oz) shredded suet
  2 tablespoons brandy
  grated rind and juice of ½ lemon
  pinch of salt
  a good pinch each of ground cinnamon, ground cloves,
     ground allspice, grated nutmeg

For the Cinnamon Cream
  150ml (¼ pint) double cream
  scant teaspoon icing sugar
  pinch of cinnamon

To Cook
1) Mix all the mincemeat ingredients together in a large
   bowl. This can then be covered and left for several
   days until needed, or be used straight away. (Because
   the mincemeat is not precooked it has a lovely fresh
   taste.)
2) Roll out the pastry to 0.3cm (⅛ in) thick and cut out
   12–15 7.5cm (3in) rounds and 12–15 6.5cm (2½in)
   rounds. Use the large rounds to line patty tins. Fill
   with the mincemeat then place the smaller rounds on
   top.
3) Cook in a pre-heated oven 220°C (425°F) Gas Mark 7
   for 15–20 minutes. Allow to cool.

To Serve
Whip up the cream with the icing sugar and cinnamon.
Raise the lid of each pie slightly and either pipe or spoon

in a little of the cream. Alternatively sprinkle the pies with a little caster sugar and hand the cream separately.

OLD-FASHIONED FISH PIE*

Serves 4–6
 600 g (1½ lb) white fish
 milk
 pinch of salt
 300ml (½ pint) parsley sauce (see Basic Preparations,
 page 149)
 800g (2 lb) cooked potatoes
 50g (2 oz) butter
 a little milk *or* cream
 grated nutmeg

For Garnish
 lemon wedges, fresh parsley

To Cook
1) Put the fish into a saucepan with enough milk to cover and a pinch of salt. Cover and bring slowly to the boil. Remove from the heat and allow to stand, covered, for 5 minutes.
2) Drain the fish (½ pint of this liquid could be used for the sauce). Skin and flake the fish, remove any bones.
3) Put the flaked fish into a deep pie dish. Pour over the parsley sauce.
4) Mash the potatoes with the butter, milk or cream and a little grated nutmeg. Check for seasoning then pipe or spoon on top of the fish mixture and cook in a pre-heated oven 200°C (400°F) Gas Mark 6 for about 30 minutes, until browned and heated through.

To Serve
Decorate with 1 or 2 sprigs of fresh parsley and lemon wedges and serve straight from the baking dish.

TANGERINE MOUSSE*

Serves 4–6
  1 sachet of gelatine
  2 tablespoons cold water
  3 whole eggs and 2 egg yolks
  75g (3 oz) caster sugar
  150ml (¼ pint) tangerine juice plus juice of 1 lemon
  grated rind of 4 tangerines
  150ml (¼ pint) double cream

To Cook
1) Place the gelatine and the water in a cup and set aside for 5 minutes.
2) Separate the eggs. Put all the yolks into a bowl with the sugar and beat well until light, thick and creamy.
3) Put the fruit juices and rind into a pan and slowly bring to the boil. Gradually stir into the creamed egg mixture. Return to the saucepan, add the soaked gelatine and stir over a very low heat until dissolved. Set aside until the mixture begins to set.
4) Beat the egg whites until frothy; whisk the cream until it holds soft peaks. Gently fold both into the egg and fruit mixture.
5) Pour into a large serving dish or individual dishes and allow to set for several hours or overnight.

To Serve (optional)
Bitter chocolate, walnuts, double cream.
  Although this mousse is good on its own, the tangerine flavour goes particularly well with dark chocolate and the

texture lends itself to a 'nutty' garnish. To finish, pipe swirls of whipped cream on top of the mousse, sprinkle with grated chocolate and place a walnut on top of each swirl.

WATERCRESS SOUP* WITH CROUTONS

Serves 4–6
   2 bunches watercress (reserve 2 or 3 sprigs for garnish)
   25g (1 oz) butter
   1 onion, finely chopped
   1 tablespoon plain flour
   salt and freshly ground black pepper
   900ml (1½ pints) milk
   150ml (¼ pint) cream

For Croutons
   25g (1 oz) butter
   1 tablespoon vegetable oil
   2–3 slices of bread 1.25–1.8cm (½–¾in) thick and cut
      into dice
   salt

To Cook
1) Wash the watercress and chop finely. Melt the butter in a large pan, add the onion and watercress. Cover and cook gently for 10 minutes. Stir in the flour and seasonings.
2) Pour on the milk and simmer very slowly for a further 15 minutes.
3) Pass through a mouli sieve or purée in a blender and pass through a coarse strainer.
4) Add 3 tablespoons of cream and re-heat gently.
5) Heat the butter and oil together in a frying pan. When the foam subsides, add the cubes of bread and fry until

golden brown on all sides. Drain on kitchen paper and sprinkle with salt.

To Serve

Pour the hot soup into a large tureen. Swirl in the remaining cream to leave a trail of white through the pale green soup and decorate with the reserved sprigs of watercress.

Hand the croutons in a separate dish.

BAKED WHOLE HAM WITH PARSLEY SAUCE

1 whole ham 4.5–5.5 kg (10–12 lb)
2 bay leaves
10 black peppercorns
1 egg white
1 tablespoon dry mustard
2 tablespoons brown sugar
2 tablespoons breadcrumbs
parsley sauce, see Basic Preparations, page 149

For Garnish

sprigs of parsley *or* watercress

To Cook

1) Soak ham in cold water overnight. Drain. Put into a large pan, cover with water and bring to the boil. Drain again and refill with fresh water.
2) Add the bay leaves and peppercorns and simmer for 2 hours. Place the ham into a baking dish, cover with foil and continue cooking in a pre-heated oven 180°C (350°F) Gas Mark 4 to give a final cooking time of 25 minutes per lb, plus 25 minutes over.
3) Some 30 minutes before the end of the cooking time take the ham out of the oven and remove the skin.

4) Mix together the egg white, mustard and sugar and spread evenly over the ham. Sprinkle the breadcrumbs on top and return to the oven for 30 minutes.

To Serve

The ham will cut better if allowed to rest for 15 minutes after baking. Begin the carving at the knuckle end, removing a triangular section first then carving in a 'V' form along the bone, taking a slice from each side in turn. Garnish with watercress or sprigs of parsley and hand the parsley sauce separately.

DANISH CHRISTMAS PUDDING

Serves 4–6
    75g (3 oz) pudding rice
    600ml (1 pint) milk
    50g (2 oz) sugar
    50g (2 oz) chopped almonds
    1 tablespoon sherry
    2–3 drops vanilla essence
    1 whole blanched almond
    300ml (½ pint) single cream

To Cook

1) Gently simmer the rice in the milk until soft and the milk is absorbed.
2) Add the sugar, chopped almonds, sherry and vanilla to the rice and allow to cool. Cover and leave in the fridge overnight.

To Serve

Pour the pudding into a pretty serving dish. Stir in the whole almond, (it must be well hidden!) and, finally, add the cream. Traditionally whoever finds the almond receives a small prize.

ASPARAGUS FEUILLETTES WITH TOMATO AND ONION SAUCE*

Serves 6

150g (6 oz) puff pastry (frozen is most suitable)
400g (1 lb) ripe tomatoes
25g (1 oz) butter
50g (2 oz) onion, finely chopped
2 garlic cloves, 1 chopped, 1 left whole
2 sprigs fresh parsley
1 teaspoon fresh basil *or* ½ teaspoon dried basil
1 bay leaf
pinch ground coriander
salt and freshly ground black pepper
1 egg yolk
1 tablespoon sesame seeds
400g (1 lb) asparagus lightly cooked *or* 1 tin asparagus tips, drained

For Garnish

watercress or sprigs of fresh basil

To Cook

1) Roll out the pastry to 5mm (¼in) thick. Cut into 6 squares and place onto a baking tray. Refrigerate until needed.
2) Peel and chop the tomatoes.
3) Melt half the butter in a small saucepan, add the onion and the chopped garlic and cook for a few minutes until soft but not coloured.
4) Add the tomatoes, herbs and spice, season lightly and cook gently until the tomato has become a pulp.

5) Push the sauce through a fine sieve, check seasonings, set aside.
6) Brush the pastry squares with egg yolk, sprinkle with sesame seeds and bake in a pre-heated oven at 240°C (475°F) Gas Mark 9 for 7–8 minutes, until golden brown. Allow to cool slightly, then split in half.
7) Whilst the pastry is cooking melt the remaining butter in a pan, add the whole garlic clove and the asparagus and very gently warm through.
8) Re-heat the tomato sauce.

To Serve

By serving in the manner of nouvelle cuisine the pastry stays beautifully crisp. First put the sauce onto the plate, then place the bottom half of the pastry case on top of it. Add the drained asparagus next (discard the garlic clove) and finally the pastry-case top. Garnish with 1 or 2 leaves of fresh basil or watercress.

ROAST LEG OF LAMB WITH GARLIC AND PARSLEY

Serves 6

    1.5–2kg (3–4 lb) leg of lamb
    2 garlic cloves, crushed
    50g (2 oz) butter, softened
    1 tablespoon chopped parsley
    salt and freshly ground black pepper

To Cook

1) Mix the garlic, butter, parsley and seasonings together and spread over the lamb.
2) Cook on a rack in a pre-heated oven 180°C (350°F) Gas Mark 4 for 25 minutes per lb, plus 25 minutes over.

3) Allow to rest in a warm place for 15 minutes before
   carving.

To Serve

This lamb does not really need anything else but if gravy
is a 'must' pour off the excess fat and stir 1 tablespoon of
flour into the meat juices. Add a little stock or water
and simmer for 5 minutes. Check seasonings and serve
separately in a sauce boat.

DAUPHINOIS POTATOES

Serves 4–6
    1 garlic clove, cut in half
    50g (2 oz) butter
    1kg (2 lb) large waxy potatoes, peeled and sliced
    salt and freshly ground black pepper
    750ml (1¼ pints) single cream *or* milk *or* a mixture of
       the two

To Cook

1) Rub the garlic pieces around a large gratin dish, then
   butter it well.
2) Arrange the potato slices in the dish in neat layers,
   seasoning lightly.
3) Pour over the cream or milk. Dot with any remaining
   butter and bake in a pre-heated oven at 170°C (325°F)
   Gas Mark 3 for 1½–2 hours, until the potatoes are
   cooked and nicely browned.

To Serve

These potatoes are best served straight from the dish they
were cooked in.

PEAS WITH SMALL GLAZED ONIONS

Serves 4–6
   25g (1 oz) butter
   1 teaspoon sugar
   24 spring onions or shallots, peeled and trimmed
   400g (1 lb) packet frozen peas
   salt and freshly ground black pepper

To Cook
1) Melt the butter in a small pan, add the sugar and fry the onions until soft and brown.
2) In another pan cook the peas quickly in a little salted boiling water and drain.
3) Mix the peas with the onions. Add a few grindings of black pepper and check for salt.

ICED MINCEMEAT BOMBE

Serves 6–8
   2–3 tablespoons apple and brandy mincemeat (see page 35)
   1 20cm (8in) round sponge cake
   2 tablespoons brandy
   3 large egg whites
   125g (5 oz) caster sugar
   600ml (1 pint) vanilla ice-cream

To Decorate
   1 sparkler (saved from Bonfire Night)

To Cook
1) Pre-heat the oven to 240°C (475°F) Gas Mark 9.
2) Heat the mincemeat in a small pan and cook for 5 minutes.

3) Cover a board with foil. Put the cake in the middle and sprinkle with brandy.
4) Whisk the egg whites until firm, then beat in the caster sugar a tablespoonful at a time.
5) Spread the mincemeat over the cake, cover with ice-cream. Top with meringue, making sure the ice-cream and cake are covered completely.
6) Cook in the hot oven for 3 minutes.

To Serve
Serve straight from the oven topped, if possible, with a small sparkler.

LASAGNE*

Serves 6
   100g (4 oz) butter
   2 rashers streaky bacon, derinded and chopped
   100g (4 oz) onions
   50g (2 oz) carrots   } chopped finely
   50g (2 oz) celery
   400g (1 lb) lean minced beef
   150ml (¼ pint) red wine
   300ml (½ pint) beef stock
   397g (14 oz) canned tomatoes, chopped
   1 tablespoon tomato purée
   ½ teaspoon marjoram
   salt and freshly ground black pepper
   400g (1 lb) lasagne
   50g (2 oz) plain flour
   450ml (¾ pint) milk
   2 tablespoons double cream
   pinch ground nutmeg
   50g (2 oz) Parmesan cheese (grated)

To Cook

1) Melt half the butter in a large heavy pan, add the bacon, onion, carrot and celery and cook until soft and lightly coloured.

2) Stir in and brown the beef, breaking up any lumps with a fork. Pour over the wine, stock, tomatoes and tomato purée. Add the marjoram and season well. Bring to the boil. Turn the heat to low, cover and simmer gently for 30–40 minutes, until the meat is tender. Check seasoning.

3) Whilst the meat is cooking, cook the lasagne and make the white sauce. For the lasagne bring a large pan of lightly salted water to the boil. Add the strips of lasagne and cook for 20–30 minutes. The pasta should retain some bite when cooked.

4) For the white sauce, melt the remaining butter in a small pan. Add the flour, cook for 2 minutes stirring well; do not allow to brown. Take from the heat and stir in the milk and cream. Beat with a wire whisk until smooth. Return to low heat whisking all the time. When the sauce comes just to the boil reduce the heat and simmer for 2–3 minutes. Allow to cool slightly then season with salt and nutmeg and stir in about three-quarters of the cheese.

5) To assemble the lasagne, butter a 20 × 30cm (8 × 12in) oven–table dish. Spread about 6mm (¼in) beef sauce over the bottom, mask with the white sauce then cover with one-third of the lasagne, overlapping slightly at the edges. Repeat the process twice more, then finish with a layer of white sauce. Sprinkle over the remaining cheese and bake for 30 minutes at 180°C (350°F) Gas Mark 4.

To Prepare in Advance

If you would like to freeze the lasagne omit the final cooking stage and freeze after assembly. When cooking straight from frozen the cooking time will need to be extended by about 20 minutes.

This dish could also be prepared and assembled in advance and left in the fridge overnight to be cooked through when needed on the following day.

To Serve
Serve browned and bubbling straight from the oven in the dish it was cooked in.

HOT HERB LOAF

100g (4 oz) butter, softened
1 teaspoon dried mixed herbs
1 tablespoon freshly chopped parsley
1 clove garlic, crushed
salt and freshly ground black pepper
1 French loaf

To Cook
1) Beat the butter until creamy, add the herbs and garlic and season lightly.
2) Cut the loaf in 2.5cm (1in) sections *without* cutting through the base of the loaf.
3) Carefully spread each cut surface with the butter. Wrap the loaf completely in foil (shiny side inwards).
4) Cook in the oven for 10–15 minutes, at 180°C (350°F) Gas Mark 4.

To Serve
Unwrap and serve straight from the oven in a basket lined with a paper kitchen towel or napkin to catch any dripping butter.

BRANDY MINCEMEAT FLAN*

Serves 6
   150g (6 oz) shortcrust pastry (ie made with 100g (4 oz)
      flour and 50g (2 oz) fat – see Basic Preparations, page
      151)
   75g (3 oz) currants ⎫
   75g (3 oz) sultanas ⎬   washed and dried
   75g (3 oz) raisins ⎭
   75g (3 oz) suet, shredded
   75g (3 oz) soft brown sugar
   200g (8 oz) apples, peeled, cored and diced small
   juice and grated rind of 1 small lemon
   1 wineglass brandy
   1 level teaspoon each of cinnamon, nutmeg, all spice,
      mixed together

For Garnish
   sprig of holly, 1 tablespoon brandy

To Cook
1) Mix all the mincemeat ingredients together.
2) Roll out the pastry to cover a 25cm (9½in) metal flan
   dish. Reserve the trimmings to decorate.
3) Spoon the mincemeat into the pastry case and decorate
   with the trimmings, perhaps cut into Christmas tree
   shapes and sprinkled with sugar.
4) Cook for 40–45 minutes in a pre-heated oven at 200°C
   (400°F) Gas Mark 6 until the pastry is brown and crisp.

To Serve
Put a sprig of holly in the centre of the flan then gently
warm 1 tablespoon of brandy, pour over the flan, light
and bring to the table with the blue flames flickering.
Brandy butter or fresh whipped cream are lovely with
this flan.

CARBONNADE DE BOEUF DE FLAMANDE*

Serves 4–6
   25g (1 oz) butter
   1 tablespoon olive oil
   600g (1½ lb) chuck steak, trimmed and cut into 5 cm
      (2in) pieces
   bouquet garni (4 stalks of parsley plus 1 bay leaf)
   400g (1 lb) onions, sliced
   1 clove garlic, crushed
   25g (1 oz) flour
   300ml (½ pint) beer
   300ml (½ pint) beef stock
   1 teaspoon sugar
   1½ teaspoons vinegar
   ½ teaspoon thyme
   salt and freshly ground black pepper

For Garnish
freshly chopped parsley

To Cook
1)   Melt the butter in the oil in a large heavy pan. Brown
     all the meat a few pieces at a time, placing the chunks
     in a large casserole dish when browned. Bury the
     bouquet garni in the meat.
2)   When all the meat is browned, fry the onions and
     garlic in the fat until well browned and soft. Stir the
     flour into the onions to absorb the fat then slowly add
     the beer and stock, stirring until well blended. Add the
     sugar, vinegar, thyme and season well. Bring to the
     boil and simmer for 1 minute.
3)   Pour the sauce over the meat (the meat should be just
     covered by the sauce), add a little more beer or stock if
     needed. Cover and cook in the oven at 180°C (350°F)
     Gas Mark 4 for 2 hours until the meat is very tender.

To Serve
Serve straight from the cooking pot sprinkled with fresh parsley and oven–baked mashed potatoes (see following recipe).

OVEN-BAKED MASHED POTATOES

Serves 4–6
  800g (2 lb) potatoes, peeled
  150ml (¼ pint) milk
  150ml (¼ pint) cream
  50g (2 oz) butter
  salt and freshly ground black pepper

To Cook
1) Boil the potatoes until tender in lightly salted water.
2) Mash the potatoes with the milk, cream and butter. Season to taste.
3) Turn into a buttered ovenproof dish, decorating the top of the potato with a fork or piping. Dot with butter. Cover tightly and bake for 30 minutes at 180°C (350°F) Gas Mark 4, until well browned.

To Serve
Serve straight from the oven in the pot it was cooked in.

OVEN-COOKED CARROTS

Serves 4–6
  50g (2 oz) butter
  400g (1 lb) carrots, peeled and cut into 5 × 0.625 × 0.625cm (2 × ¼ × ¼in) sticks
  1 teaspoon sugar
  salt and freshly ground black pepper

For Garnish
freshly chopped parsley

To Cook
1) Melt the butter in a pan, toss in the carrots, add the sugar and seasonings and turn into an oven-proof dish. Cover and cook in the oven at 180°C (350°F) Gas Mark 4 for 1½ hours or on the oven bottom whilst something like a carbonnade is cooking.

To Serve
Usually the carrots are pretty dry but if not just drain and serve with the chopped parsley.

CHRISTMAS FRUIT SALAD

Serves 4–6
   397g (14 oz) tinned peach halves, drained
   100g (4 oz) dried apricots
   25g (1 oz) raisins
   25g (1 oz) sultanas
   25g (1 oz) soft brown sugar
   1 tablespoon clear honey
   juice of 2 lemons
   1 teaspoon each cinnamon, nutmeg, allspice, mixed
      together
   2 cloves
   1 tablespoon brandy

To Cook
1) Mix everything together. Put into an ovenproof dish and bake for 1–2 hours at 180°C (350°F) Gas Mark 4.

To Serve
Turn into a pretty warmed serving dish.

LOBSTER NEWBURG

Serves 2
  1 lobster, cooked
  50g (2 oz) butter
  salt, grated nutmeg and cayenne pepper
  250ml (⅜ pint) double cream
  4 egg yolks
  2 tablespoons brandy
  2 tablespoons dry sherry

For Garnish
  fresh parsley sprigs or watercress, and lemon wedges

To Cook
1) Prepare the lobster by first twisting off the claws, then halve it by inserting the point of a sharp knife into the first neck section and cutting straight down to the tail. Turn the lobster and cut through the head.
2) Discard the sac which is to be found behind the eyes. Extract all the meat and chop neatly into small pieces. Strip out the browny coloured gills, discard, then wash the shells thoroughly.
3) Crack the claws, being careful not to leave any small splinters of shell on the meat. Cut the meat into small pieces.
4) Melt the butter in a frying pan, add the lobster pieces and sprinkle with a little salt, nutmeg and cayenne pepper. Cook for 1 minute.
5) Beat together the cream and egg yolks and pour into the pan. When the mixture thickens slightly pour in the brandy and sherry.
6) Check seasoning and spoon the mixture into the reserved lobster shells.

To Serve
Garnish with fresh parsley sprigs or watercress and the
lemon wedges.

GREEN SALAD

Mix together any of the following vegetables and dress
with a light vinaigrette (see Basic Preparations, page 150)

Chinese leaves ⎫
crisp lettuce   ⎬   shredded
white cabbage ⎭
green pepper, seeded and chopped
cucumber   ⎫
spring onions   ⎪
chives   ⎬   chopped
parsley   ⎭

MIXED SORBETS* WITH CHAMPAGNE

300ml (½ pint) water
200g (8 oz) caster sugar
juice of 1 lemon
400g (1 lb) mixed fruit purées; unsweetened raspberries,
   blackcurrants, pineapples, strawberries and
   gooseberries are all suitable
2 egg whites

To Make
1) Stir the water, sugar and lemon juice over a low heat
   until the sugar dissolves.
2) Divide the syrup between the individual fruit purées,
   and mix each well. Put into individual containers

suitable for the freezer and freeze uncovered until 'slushy'.

3) Stiffly whisk the egg whites, divide equally between the sorbets beating each one until thick and light.

4) Return all to the freezer; when set firm cover tightly.

To Serve

Scoop different balls of sorbet into a sundae glass. Pour over a little champagne and serve immediately.

If you have some small glasses you could put a tiny amount of sorbet into each glass and serve all the glasses together on a plate. This looks spectacular but can present problems carrying them!

Timetables

The timetables are worked out to give various 'sitting-down' times. Any adjustments can be made lightly in pencil then erased once used.

To work out the 'start time' calculate the exact cooking time for the main dish from the times given in the recipe or time charts and add on 20 minutes to cover resting and last-minute preparations. Subtract this figure from the 'sitting-down' time (8 p.m. has been used in the timetables here) and enter the 'start time' in the space provided.

TIMETABLE FOR MENU NO. 3

Watercress Soup with Croutons

. . .

Baked Whole Ham with Parsley Sauce,
New Potatoes, Calabrese

. . .

Danish Christmas Pudding

The Day Before
Soak ham.
Make pudding.
If soup is already made and frozen, take out of freezer.

During the Morning
Prepare soup up to re-heating stage (step 4).
Fry croutons.
Scrub potatoes.
Trim calabrese.

Start Time .... p.m.
Drain ham and commence cooking.
7.10 p.m. Skin ham and cover with glaze. Put back into oven.

To Finish Cooking

7.25 p.m.   Put potatoes on to simmer.

7.40 p.m.   Make parsley sauce, leave to simmer, stirring occasionally.

7.45 p.m.   Take out ham and allow to rest in a warm place.
Put plates to warm.

7.50 p.m.   Warm soup through gently, place croutons in oven.

7.55 p.m.   Put lightly salted water on to boil for calabrese.

8.00 p.m.   Put calabrese on to simmer, serve soup and croutons.
Take pudding from fridge. Stir in the single whole almond.

After soup course, drain and serve vegetables, carve ham, put sauce into sauce-boat.

TIMETABLE FOR MENU NO. 4

Asparagus Feuillettes with Tomato and Onion Sauce

. . .

Roast Leg of Lamb with Garlic and Parsley, Dauphinois Potatoes, Peas with Small Glazed Onions

. . .

Iced Mincemeat Bombe

The Day Before
Make sponge cake.
Make apple and brandy mincemeat.
Take pastry from freezer.

During the Morning
Make the tomato sauce.
Cook fresh asparagus (if using).
Make up butter mixture and spread over lamb.
Prepare onions.
Roll out pastry.

Start Time .... p.m.
Put lamb in pre-heated oven; prepare potatoes, put in oven on low shelf.

To Finish Cooking
7.30 p.m.   Cook onions. Assemble pudding up to ice-cream stage.
7.35 p.m.   Cook peas, drain. Brush pastry with egg yolk and sprinkle on seeds.
7.45 p.m.   Take lamb from oven, leave to rest in a warm place.
             Put plates to warm.
7.50 p.m.   Cook pastry cases, warm sauce and asparagus gently.
             Make gravy if needed.
8.00 p.m.   Add onions to peas and put to warm through gently, assemble and serve feuillettes.

After first course, serve potatoes straight from the oven (turn temperature up ready for the Bombe). Serve peas, carve lamb. After second course whip up meringue, finish and cook Bombe.

Christmas Day

Unless you go out for lunch it has to be accepted that part of the big day will be spent in the kitchen! Our menus are simple and easily prepared so this 'kitchen time' will be kept to a minimum. Several dishes can be made in advance with no loss of quality. Unless it is essential to have frozen, our advice is to buy a fresh bird. If you have a frozen bird remember to take it out of the freezer the day before it's needed; it must be defrosted completely before being cooked.

Consider having the main meal later in the day. Many cooks find the thought of preparing a traditional Christmas lunch, complete with trimmings, for a 1.00 p.m. start very daunting. We find that having the meal later takes a lot of pressure off the cook and gives more time for playing with new toys, going out for a walk or to church, or just relaxing between visits to the kitchen to check progress. Sloe gin will warm you up on your return – the recipe is in the Basic Preparations section (page 150)!

The most common mistake made when cooking a meal with many different items is to put the vegetables on far too early and then allow them to sit in the cooking water until needed. Using our timetables will make sure this doesn't happen; if you change any of the dishes, just make any necessary adjustments.

Although the timetables are given for the menus listed, they can, as indicated above, be easily adjusted should you wish to use different starters, vegetables or sweets. Try to plan the meal in good time but don't be too rigid; sometimes an impromptu addition or deletion can make a meal really memorable.

Our advice is to buy a fresh bird

The starters we have given need very little in the way of final preparation and will leave you free to concentrate on the main course. Just take your aperitif into the kitchen, put on your prettiest apron and relax – it will all be delicious!

TABLE SETTINGS

Try to give the table setting a bit of planning too; it seems a shame to take your lovely meal to an ordinarily laid table. Place-cards, candles, crackers and napkins can all be used to great effect. Home-made crackers are good because a small present can be chosen especially for each person sitting down to the meal. If you have a separate dining room it's a nice idea not to allow anyone in until you are ready and then surprise them.

TEA-TIME

After the main meal and the chorus of 'I couldn't eat another thing', it always comes as a surprise that a plate of sandwiches brought out during the early evening can disappear as though a plague of locusts is in the house. Now is the time to cut the Christmas cake; served with small wedges of Wensleydale cheese, it should be all you'll need!

CHRISTMAS DINNER

We suggest three different menus using the most popular of Christmas birds. Unfortunately the 'Capon' as such is no longer available because of EEC regulations. The equivalent is known as 'Big chicken' and weighs in at

Take half an hour off . . .

2.5–3kg (5–7 lb). Now although it sounds as if it goes around 'making offers you can't refuse', it is in fact exceedingly good, and with all the traditional trimmings makes a beautifully tender light alternative to turkey or goose.

Whichever you choose, do make sure you have a good sharp carving knife!

MENU 8: Roast 'Big Chicken' Menu
(See Timetable, page 72)

page

Shirley Conran Mushrooms   54
('Life is too short to stuff a mushroom!?')
· · ·

Roast 'Big Chicken'
Mint and Rosemary Stuffing★,
Sausagemeat Balls, New Potatoes,
Roast Potatoes, Brussels Sprouts
with Bacon Snippets, Cranberry
Jelly, Gravy   55–8
· · ·

Light Christmas Pudding   58
Fluffy Orange Sauce   59
· · ·

Stilton, Nuts and Fresh Fruit
· · ·

Coffee

MENU 9: Roast Turkey Menu
(See Timetable, page 74)

page

Smoked Salmon Rolls Stuffed with
Prawns   59
· · ·

Warm Vichysoisse with Cream   60
· · ·

French Roast Turkey, Celery and
Apple Stuffing, Roast Potatoes,
Creamed Potatoes, Glazed Carrots,
Bread Sauce, Cranberry Sauce,
Forcemeat, Broccoli Spears, Bacon
and Chipolata Rolls, Gravy   61–4

· · ·

· · ·

Stilton, Nuts and Fresh Fruit
· · ·

Coffee

MENU 10: **Roast Goose Menu**
(See Timetable, page 75)

· · ·

Stilton, Nuts and Fresh Fruit
· · ·

Coffee

FORCEMEATS AND STUFFINGS

Several good recipes for forcemeats and stuffings are given in this section, but it is possible to experiment with confidence using the chart below. A good forcemeat should be a subtle blend of flavours with no one ingredient dominant, so special care must be taken when using lemon juice or thyme not to overpower the other ingredients.

Herbs	*Bulk*	*Spices*
Parsley	Ham or Bacon	Salt
Thyme	Suet	Pepper
Tarragon	Oysters	Nutmeg
Winter Savory	Anchovy	Cloves
Marjoram	Breadcrumbs	Mace
Basil	Soaked bread	Garlic
	Dried apricots	Shallots
	Celery	Chives
	Onions	
	Chestnuts	
	Walnuts	

Choose a combination of ingredients from each column, mix together with beaten egg, and use to stuff the bird in the normal way.

Oven Roasting Chart For Christmas Poultry

BIRD	WEIGHT	TIME
Turkey	4–5kg (12–14 lb)	15 minutes per pound
Goose	3–4kg (8–10 lb)	15 minutes per pound
'Big Chicken'	2–3kg (5–7 lb)	20 minutes per pound plus 20 minutes

To test if the bird is done pierce the thigh with a skewer. If clear juices run out the bird is ready; if the juices are pink, continue cooking for 15 minutes longer.

Recipes

SHIRLEY CONRAN MUSHROOMS

Serves 6–8
   150ml (¼ pint) white sauce (see Basic Preparations,
      page 149)
   1 tablespoon cooked ham, cut into small dice
   1 tablespoon grated cheese
   salt and freshly ground black pepper
   3–4 button mushrooms per person, 2.5–3.75cm
      (1–1½in) maximum in diameter
   flour to coat
   1 large egg beaten with 2 tablespoons milk
   100g (4 oz) fresh brown breadcrumbs
   oil to deep fry

For Garnish
   lemon wedges and watercress

To Cook
1) Make up the white sauce, stir in the ham and cheese,
   season and allow to cool.
2) Wipe the mushrooms and pull out the stalks. Using a
   teaspoon fill each mushroom cup with the cold sauce.
3) Toss the mushrooms in the flour, then in the egg
   wash, then roll in the breadcrumbs.
4) Deep-fry in the *hot oil* until golden brown and crisp,
   1–2 minutes.

To Serve
Serve with lemon wedges and watercress.

N.B. The mushrooms can be stuffed and breadcrumbed
well in advance and kept cool until needed.

ROAST 'BIG CHICKEN'

Now that caponizing by injection has been banned by the EEC, the nearest equivalent will be a big chicken of around 2–3kg (5–7 lb) in weight. Careful roasting and interesting stuffing, however, will make sure that this bird is every bit as festive as the capons were; indeed, many people may prefer the less fatty, more delicate flavour.

    2–3kg (5–7 lb) 'Big Chicken'
    stuffing for neck end
    forcemeat for cavity (see page 56)
    50g (2 oz) butter
    2 rashers streaky bacon
    1 onion, peeled but whole
    300ml (½ pint) stock (made from the giblets)
    1 tablespoon flour
    1 tablespoon dry sherry (optional)

For Garnish
    watercress and leg frills

To Cook
1) Stuff the chicken at both ends securing the neck flap with a skewer if necessary and trussing tightly.
2) Rub the bird well with the butter and cover with the bacon rashers.
3) Place into a large roasting tin with the whole onion and the stock.
4) Cover with foil (shiny side towards the bird) and roast in a preheated oven, 180°C (350°F) Gas Mark 4 for the time shown on the chart (page 53). Take off the foil half an hour before the end of the cooking time in order to brown the bird.

5) Take the bird from the roasting tin, put to rest in a warm place whilst you prepare the gravy.
6) Skim off as much fat from the stock as possible. Pour off the stock and reserve, leaving a small amount in the bottom of the tin. Stir in the flour and cook for 2 minutes. Slowly re-add the stock, whisking well. Check seasonings; if liked, add tablespoon of dry sherry.

To Serve

Put the chicken on a large platter. Place the frills on the legs and the watercress to one side. If there is enough room put the sausagemeat balls around as well. Carve at the table.

MINT AND ROSEMARY STUFFING*

Enough to stuff one 4kg (10 lb) bird
    50g (2 oz) butter
    2 sticks celery
    200g (8 oz) onion } finely chopped
    200g (8 oz) fresh breadcrumbs
    2 teaspoons dried rosemary
    2 tablespoons mint sauce
    rind of 1 lemon, grated
    1 large egg, beaten
    salt and freshly ground black pepper

To Cook

1) Melt the butter in a frying pan and cook the celery and onion until soft but not coloured.
2) Mix the breadcrumbs with the herbs, mint sauce and lemon rind, add the cooled onions and celery and bind together with the beaten egg. Season.

N.B. This stuffing can be made up and frozen if required. Follow the above instructions but do not add the egg until just before stuffing the bird.

SAUSAGEMEAT BALLS

25g (1 oz) butter
2 sticks of celery
1 onion } finely chopped
400g (1 lb) sausagemeat
½ teaspoon mixed herbs
salt and freshly ground black pepper

To Cook
1) Melt the butter in a frying pan and cook the celery and onion until soft but not coloured.
2) Mash the sausagemeat with a fork. Mix in the onion and celery followed by the herbs and seasoning.
3) Form into balls about 4cm (1½in) in diameter and bake at 180°C (350°F) Gas Mark 4 for 30–40 minutes.

To Serve
Place the sausagemeat balls around the bird, interspaced with watercress or roast potatoes.

CRANBERRY JELLY

1.25kg (3 lb) cranberries
600ml (1 pint) water
sugar (see method below for quantity)

To Cook
1) Put the cranberries and water into a large pan and simmer gently until the berries have popped and are mushy.

2) Strain through a jelly cloth and measure the purée.
   Return to the pan with 400g (1 lb) of sugar per 600ml
   (1 pint) of purée.
3) Stir over a low heat until the sugar dissolves then boil
   quickly to a jelly state. Skim off the froth and turn the
   jelly into warmed jam jars. Seal and store until needed.

LIGHT CHRISTMAS PUDDING

Serves 6–8
   400g (1 lb) plain flour
   pinch of salt
   4 eggs
   150ml (¼ pint) milk
   250g (10 oz) raisins
   150g (6 oz) currants
   pinch of grated nutmeg
   grated rind of 1 lemon

For Garnish
   sprig of holly, 1 tablespoon brandy (optional)

To Cook
1) Make a batter with the flour, salt, eggs and milk. Add
   the fruit, nutmeg and lemon rind, and a little more
   milk if the mixture looks too dry.
2) Turn into a greased pudding basin, cover with greaseproof paper and foil and steam or boil for 5 hours.
3) Allow to cool. Wrap and store until needed.

To Re-heat
Steam or boil for 2 hours.

To Serve
Serve garnished with holly and fluffy orange sauce. If you
would like to flame the pudding as you serve it, warm 1

tablespoon of brandy, pour over and light just at the point of serving.

FLUFFY ORANGE SAUCE

Serves 6–8
   25g (2 oz) butter
   100g (4 oz) icing sugar
   2 large eggs
   2 tablespoons Cointreau or Grand Marnier
   150ml (¼ pint) double cream

To Cook
1) Cream the butter and sugar. Separate the eggs and beat the yolks into the mixture. Stir in the liqueur and cream.
2) Heat slowly in a double pan until the mixture thickens stirring all the time.
3) Beat the egg whites until just stiff. Whisk into the custard and serve.

SMOKED SALMON ROLLS STUFFED WITH PRAWNS

Serves 6
   50g (2 oz) mayonnaise
   juice of ½ lemon
   1 tablespoon mixed chopped fresh herbs or parsley
   200g (8 oz) prawns, shelled
   salt and cayenne pepper
   6 slices of smoked salmon

For Garnish
   watercress and lemon wedges

To Make

1) Mix together the mayonnaise, lemon juice and herbs. Toss in the prawns and season.
2) Put a slice of smoked salmon on each plate. Spoon some prawn mixture into the centre and roll up.

To Serve

Garnish each plate with watercress and 2 wedges of lemon (one placed on either side of the roll helps to keep the salmon in place).

VICHYSOISSE (WARM) WITH CREAM

Serves 6–8

    400g (1 lb) potatoes, peeled and chopped
    400g (1 lb) leeks, trimmed, cleaned and sliced
    1.8 litres (3 pints) chicken stock
    salt

For Garnish

    double cream, freshly chopped chives or parsley

To Cook

1) Put the potatoes, leeks, stock and a little salt into a large pan and simmer for 45 minutes. The vegetables should be well cooked.
2) Press the soup through a mouli sieve or blend in a liquidizer and then sieve; check seasoning.

To Serve

Pour the soup into a warmed tureen – any large pot will do. Tie a red ribbon around the outside to give a festive look and serve hot with the double cream swirled across the top and a sprinkling of chopped chives or parsley.

FRENCH ROAST TURKEY

4–5kg (10–14 lb) turkey, oven ready
forcemeat
stuffing
100g (4 oz) butter
4 rashers bacon
1 onion, peeled but left whole
300–600ml (½–1 pint) giblet stock
1 tablespoon flour
salt and freshly ground black pepper
sherry or brandy (optional)

For Garnish
leg frills, watercress or parsley

To Cook
1) Stuff the turkey at both ends, using a forcemeat at one
   end and stuffing at the other. Secure the neck flap with
   a skewer and truss tightly.
2) Rub butter all over the breast and legs and place the
   bacon rashers over the breast.
3) Put into a roasting tin with the onion and about 300ml
   (½ pint) of stock. Cover with foil (shiny side down).
4) Roast in a preheated oven at 180°C (350°F) Gas Mark
   4, using the oven chart (page 53) as a guide to timing.
   Take the foil off the bird 30 minutes before the end of
   cooking time in order to brown the bird.
5) Set the bird in a warm place to rest whilst you make
   the gravy.
6) Skim the fat from the roasting tin. Pour off and reserve
   the stock. Sprinkle the flour over the bottom of the
   tin, scraping in any bits that cling to the tin. Cook for
   1–2 minutes; add the stock slowly, whisking all the
   time, and simmer for a few minutes. Check for seasoning; add a tablespoon of sherry or brandy if liked.

To Serve

Put the bird onto a large serving platter, place the frills on the legs and surround with roast potatoes and bacon and chipolata rolls. Decorate with watercress or parsley. Carve at the table and hand the gravy separately in a sauce boat.

CELERY AND APPLE STUFFING

50g (2 oz) butter
100g (4 oz) onion ⎫
3 sticks celery ⎭ finely chopped
100g (4 oz) cooking apples, peeled, cored and chopped
150g (6 oz) fresh breadcrumbs
1 teaspoon sage
grated rind of 1 lemon
salt and freshly ground black pepper
1 egg, beaten

To Cook

1) Melt the butter in a frying pan and cook the onion and celery until soft but not brown.
2) Add the apple and cook for 1–2 minutes. Remove from the heat.
3) Stir in the breadcrumbs, sage and lemon rind. Season and bind with egg.

BREAD SAUCE

2 cloves
1 onion
½ teaspoon mace
450ml (¾ pint) milk
3–4 tablespoons white breadcrumbs

salt and freshly ground black pepper
small knob of butter

To Cook

1) Stick the cloves into the onion and put into a pan with the mace and milk, cover and simmer over a very gentle heat for 10 minutes.
2) Remove the onion and stir in the breadcrumbs; simmer gently for 5 minutes until the sauce thickens.
3) Season with salt and pepper and beat in the butter. Serve at once.

CRANBERRY SAUCE

200g (8 oz) fresh cranberries
150g (6 oz) sugar
150ml (¼ pint) water
1 teaspoon grated orange rind

To Cook

1) Put the cranberries, sugar and water into a heavy-based pan and bring to the boil, stirring all the time.
2) Simmer gently over a low heat until the skins of the cranberries pop. Do not overcook.
3) Stir in the orange rind and set aside to cool. Store in the fridge until needed.

To Serve

Put into a pretty dish and serve cold.

FORCEMEAT

75g (3 oz) lean bacon, derinded and finely chopped
100g (4 oz) beef suet, shredded

grated rind of ½ lemon
1 teaspoon chopped parsley
½ teaspoon chopped thyme
½ teaspoon chopped oregano
good pinch of grated nutmeg
salt and freshly ground black pepper
2 eggs, beaten

To Make

Mix all dry ingredients together well and then bind with beaten egg.

BACON AND CHIPOLATA ROLLS

6 chipolata sausages
3 rashers bacon

To Cook

1) Derind the bacon and cut each rasher in half lengthways. Roll the bacon pieces around the sausages and secure with a cocktail stick.
2) Bake for 20–30 minutes at 180°C (350°F) Gas Mark 4, until the bacon is crisp and brown.

To Serve

Arrange around the bird on a large serving platter interspaced with roast potatoes and watercress or parsley.

PLUM PUDDING

Serves 6–8

200g (8 oz) beef suet, shredded
200g (8 oz) breadcrumbs
150g (6 oz) plain flour

150g (6 oz) currants } washed and dried
400g (1 lb) raisins
150g (6 oz) orange and lemon peel
good pinch each of ground ginger and grated nutmeg
6 eggs, beaten
wineglass of brandy

For Garnish
sprig of holly, 1 tablespoon brandy

To Cook
1) Mix the suet with the breadcrumbs and flour, add the currants, raisins, mixed peel and spices.
2) Stir in the eggs and brandy, and mix thoroughly.
3) Put into a buttered pudding basin and cover tightly with greaseproof paper then foil. Steam or boil for 6 hours.
4) Allow to cool. Keep in a cool place until needed.

To Re-heat
Steam or boil for 2 hours.

To Serve
Put a sprig of holly on top; gently warm 1 tablespoon of brandy, pour over and light just as you take the pudding to the table. Hand the Drambuie Sauce separately.

DRAMBUIE SAUCE

Serves 6–8
50g (2 oz) butter
50g (2 oz) cornflour
600 ml (1 pint) milk
50g (2 oz) caster sugar
2 tablespoons Drambuie

To Cook

1) Melt the butter over a low heat and stir in the cornflour. Cook without browning for 2 minutes.
2) Take from the heat and slowly stir in the milk.
3) Bring to the boil, whisking all the time, then add the sugar and Drambuie. Simmer for 2 minutes. Check for sweetness and serve.

MELON SALAD

Serves 4–6
   ½ cucumber
   1 ripe melon
   2 tomatoes
   2 spring onions
   1 tablespoon chopped parsley
   2 tablespoons light vinaigrette (see Basic Preparations, page 150)
   1 teaspoon sugar

For Garnish
   freshly chopped parsley

To Make

1) Peel the cucumber and dice the flesh. Sprinkle with salt and leave for 30 minutes.
2) Cut up the melon into small balls or dice, discarding the pips and outer skin.
3) Peel the tomatoes by placing in boiling water for 1 minute then plunging into cold water. Discard the skins and seeds and chop the flesh roughly.
4) Trim and slice the spring onions.
5) Rinse the cucumber and dry well. Mix all the vegetables with the melon and parsley. Stir in the vinaigrette, adding sugar to taste.

To Serve
The salad looks prettiest served in glass sundae dishes with a little more freshly chopped parsley sprinkled on top.

ONION SOUP WITH A PUFF PASTRY CRUST

Serves 4
   25g (1 oz) butter
   2 large onions, sliced
   1.5 litres (2½ pints) chicken stock
   good pinch dried thyme
   salt and freshly ground black pepper
   370g (13 oz) puff pastry (frozen is most suitable)
   250g (10 oz) Gruyère cheese, grated
   1 egg, beaten

To Cook
1) Melt the butter in a large heavy pan and sauté the onions until soft and very brown.
2) Add the chicken stock, thyme and season well. Simmer for 30–40 minutes.
3) Select four suitable ovenproof soup cups; roll out the pastry and cut into four circles a little larger than each soup cup.
4) Take half the cheese and divide it equally between the cups. Pour the soup over the cheese. Brush the outer edges of each cup with beaten egg. Cover each with pastry and seal down. Sprinkle with the remaining cheese and bake for 6–7 minutes at 190°C (375°F) Gas Mark 5, until well browned.

To Serve
Serve straight from the oven in the soup cups. If the soup has bubbled over too much, simply tie a large paper napkin around each cup.

ROAST GOOSE

3½–4kg (8–10 lb) goose, oven ready
potato stuffing
50g (2 oz) butter
1 onion, peeled but left whole
300ml (½ pint) giblet stock
1 tablespoon flour
lemon juice
mushroom ketchup

For Garnish
leg frills, watercress or parsley

To Cook
1) Stuff the goose and truss tightly.
2) Rub butter over the skin and place on a rack in a roasting tin. Put in the onion and pour over the stock.
3) Cover with foil and roast in a pre-heated oven 180°C (350°F) Gas Mark 4 as per the time chart (page 53). Take the goose out of the roasting tin and set to rest in a warm place.
4) To make the gravy, first pour off the fat from the roasting tin. Skim and reserve the stock. Sprinkle the flour into the tin and cook for 2 minutes, scraping in any bits that cling to the tin. Return the stock and boil for 2 minutes. Add the lemon juice and mushroom ketchup to taste.

To Serve
Put the goose onto a large serving platter and arrange the leg frills. Surround with roast potatoes and decorate with some watercress or parsley. Carve at the table. Hand the gravy and apple sauce separately.

POTATO STUFFING

400g (1 lb) potatoes
25g (1 oz) butter
1 large onion, finely chopped
½ teaspoon dried marjoram
50g (2 oz) parsley, chopped
salt and freshly ground black pepper

To Cook
1) Peel and dice the potatoes. Cook in lightly salted water for 6 minutes, drain and dry well on kitchen roll.
2) Melt the butter and fry the onion until soft but not brown. Add the herbs and potato dice. Season and mix well.

APPLE SAUCE*

25g (1 oz) butter
400g (1 lb) cooking apples, peeled, cored and sliced
sugar, lemon juice, grated nutmeg to taste

To Cook
1) Melt the butter in a medium-sized pan over low heat, add the apple, cover tightly and gently cook for 5 minutes.
2) Allow the mixture to cool then mash thoroughly, adding the sugar, lemon juice and nutmeg to taste.

ANOTHER CHRISTMAS PUDDING

Serves 6–8
200g (8 oz) suet, shredded
150g (6 oz) breadcrumbs

½ teaspoon grated nutmeg
200g (8 oz) raisins
200g (8 oz) currants   } washed and dried
50g (2 oz) sultanas
150g (6 oz) candied orange and lemon peel
5 eggs, beaten
1 wineglass brandy
300ml (½ pint) milk

For Garnish
sprig of holly, 1 tablespoon brandy

To Cook
1) Mix the suet, breadcrumbs and nutmeg together. Add the fruit and candied peel and mix again.
2) Pour over the eggs, brandy and milk and mix well.
3) Put the mixture into a basin, cover with greaseproof paper then foil, tie securely and boil for 5 hours.
4) Store, covered, in a cool place until needed.

To Re-heat
Boil or steam for a further 2 hours.

To Serve
Put a sprig of holly in the top of the pudding. Gently heat 1 tablespoon of brandy and pour over; light just as you take the pudding to the table. Hand the brandy butter or sauce separately.

BRANDY SAUCE

Serves 6–8
   25g (1 oz) cornflour
   50g (2 oz) caster sugar
   glass of white wine

juice of ½ lemon
300ml (½ pint) water
brandy or rum to taste

To Cook

1) Mix the cornflour with a little water until smooth.
2) Put all the other ingredients except the brandy into a pan; heat, stirring quickly, until the mixture starts to boil. Add the cornflour and brandy then beat until smooth and the mixture thickens slightly.
3) Turn into a warmed sauceboat and serve separately.

BRANDY BUTTER

100g (4 oz) caster sugar
100g (4 oz) butter
1 wineglass brandy

To Make

Cream the sugar and butter until light and fluffy. Beat in the brandy. Chill until needed.

Timetables

These timetables are worked out to give a 2 p.m. sitting-down time. Start time can be worked out by calculating the cooking time using the chart provided and adding 20 minutes resting time.

TIMETABLE FOR MENU NO. 8

Shirley Conran Mushrooms

· · ·

Roast 'Big Chicken', Mint and Rosemary Stuffing, Sausagemeat Balls, New Potatoes, Roast Potatoes, Brussels Sprouts with Bacon Snippets, Cranberry Jelly, Gravy

· · ·

Light Christmas Pudding
Fluffy Orange Sauce

· · ·

Stilton, Nuts, Fruit

· · ·

Coffee

2–3 Weeks Ahead
Make up and freeze Mint and Rosemary Stuffing.
Make up and Store Light Christmas Pudding and Cranberry Jelly.

The Day Before
Prepare mushrooms up to cooking stage. Refrigerate.
Make stuffing (if not frozen). Stuff and truss bird.

Start Time .... a.m.
Put bird in oven.

During the Morning

Prepare vegetables.
Par-boil potatoes for roasting.
Grill bacon rashers until crispy and chop up small for sprout garnish.
Set table, put out cranberry sauce.
Arrange cheese, wash celery and put nuts and fruit into a basket.
Put out coffee cups.

To Finish Cooking

12.15 p.m.	Put pudding on to steam.
1.15 p.m.	Melt dripping in a roasting tin and put in potatoes for roasting. Place in oven.
1.30 p.m.	Put sausagemeat balls in oven. Adjust shelves after bird is taken out.
1.40 p.m.	Put new potatoes on to cook. Take bird from oven and keep warm. Put plates to warm. Start to make gravy.
1.50 p.m.	Put on water for sprouts, salt lightly and when boiling cook sprouts until almost tender – 5–6 minutes. Drain, cover and keep warm.
1.52 p.m.	Start fluffy sauce but don't beat egg whites yet.
1.58 p.m.	Deep-fry mushrooms and serve.

After the First Course

Carve the Big Chicken and serve with the stuffing and sausagemeat balls. Dish up and serve the roast potatoes, new potatoes and sprouts adding the crispy bacon pieces. Check seasoning of gravy and serve separately.

Let everyone have a breather after the main course while you finish the fluffy sauce.

TIMETABLE FOR MENU NO. 9

Smoked Salmon Rolls stuffed with Prawns

. . .

Vichysoisse (Warm) with Cream

. . .

Roast Turkey, Celery and Apple Stuffing, Roast Potatoes, Creamed Potatoes, Forcemeat, Glazed Carrots, Broccoli Spears, Cranberry Sauce, Bread Sauce, Bacon and Chipolata Rolls, Gravy

. . .

Plum Pudding, Drambuie Sauce

. . .

Stilton, Nuts, Fruit

. . .

Coffee

2–3 Weeks Ahead
Make up and boil pudding.
Make up and freeze soup.

The Day Before
Make cranberry sauce.
Make soup (if not frozen).
Make stuffing and forcemeat and stuff and truss turkey.

Start Time .... a.m.

During the Morning
Prepare vegetables.
Par-boil potatoes for roasting.

Make bread sauce.
Mix prawns with marjoram and herbs.
Make Drambuie sauce.
Put bird in oven.
Set table, put out cheese, nuts, fruits etc.
Put out coffee cups.

To Finish Cooking

12.00 noon	Put pudding on to steam.
1.15 p.m.	Put potatoes in the oven to roast.
1.30 p.m.	Put bacon rolls into oven.
	Put potatoes to be creamed on to boil.
1.40 p.m.	Take out turkey and put to keep warm.
	Put plates to warm.
1.45 p.m.	Put soup on to warm gently.
	Make up salmon rolls.
1.50 p.m.	Start gravy and allow to simmer. Put on carrots and broccoli, cook until almost tender, 5–10 minutes, drain, cover and keep warm.
2.00 p.m.	Serve salmon rolls. Check soup and gravy are OK.

After the first course serve the soup, check the gravy. After the second course, carve the turkey, dish up the roast potatoes and the bacon and chipolata rolls and place round the bird and serve. Serve the gravy, carrots, broccoli and creamed potatoes separately.

Re-heat the Drambuie sauce very gently after the main course.

TIMETABLE FOR MENU NO. 10

Melon Salad

. . .

Onion Soup with a Puff Pastry Crust

. . .

Roast Goose, Potato Stuffing, Apple
Sauce, Roast Potatoes, Braised Celery,
Savoy Cabbage

. . .

Another Christmas Pudding

. . .

Stilton, Nuts, Fruit

. . .

Coffee

2–3 Weeks Ahead
Make and boil pudding.

The Day Before
Make stuffing and stuff and truss goose.
Make apple sauce.
Make brandy butter (if using).

Start Time .... a.m.

During the Morning
Make up onion soup and cover the soup cups with pastry.
Prepare vegetables, par-boil potatoes for roasting and
celery for braising.
Make up melon salad and vinaigrette but do not combine
the two yet.
Set table, put out cheese, nuts, fruit etc. Put out apple
sauce.
Put out coffee cups.
Put bird in oven.

To Finish Cooking
12.00 noon   Put pudding on to steam.
1.15 p.m.   Put potatoes in oven to roast and celery into
              oven to braise.

1.40 p.m.	Take goose from the oven and put to keep warm. Put plates to warm.
1.50 p.m.	Start to make gravy and brandy sauce (if using).
1.55 p.m.	Put soup cups into the oven, moving celery and potatoes to the oven floor. Put on water for cabbage. Mix melon and vinaigrette together.
2.00 p.m.	Serve the melon. Check gravy, sauce and pastry.

Serve the soup after the first course. Check gravy and put the cabbage to cook. After the second course, dish up and serve the celery and cabbage. Put the roast potatoes around the goose. Carve and serve.

Finish the brandy sauce after the main course.

Boxing Day

Boxing Day is the day when a little forward planning can pay dividends. Try to choose meals that will look after themselves and offer a contrast to the Christmas dinner of the previous day. Beef or lamb are good choices for the main meal and always seem very welcome. As a change from the more traditional stuffing, we suggest filling the crown roast with a lighter mixture of rice and peas. The new potatoes and strawberries are an extravagance, of course, but then it is Christmas!

Our Danish friend Marianne makes the unusual fruit salad given here. Her sister Karina prefers it without the almond essence; either way it is absolutely delicious but, be warned, very more-ish!

MENU 11: Simple Buffet Lunch

	page
Cold Baked Ham	26
Cold Roast Turkey	61
Hot Jacket Potatoes	
Warm Rolls★	21
Green Salad	40
Mixed Salad	
Old English Trifle	84

MENU 12: Relaxed Family Dinner
(See Timetable, page 95)

	page
Baked Eggs	85

Try to choose meals that will look after themselves

. . .

Beef in Red Wine with Mushrooms★   86
Creamed Potatoes

. . .

Green Fruit Salad   87

MENU 13: Easy Boxing Day Special Dinner Party
(See Timetable, page 96)

page

Potted Shrimps   87

. . .

Crown Roast of Lamb, Baked Rice,
Peas, New Potatoes, Glazed
Carrots   88–90

. . .

Strawberry Pavlova   90

MENU 14: Another Easy Dinner Party Menu
(See Timetable, page 97)

page

Hot Stuffed Tomatoes   91

. . .

Roast Loin of Pork Dijonaise
Boulangère Potatoes, Brussels
Sprouts with Nuts   91–3

. . .

Marianne's Fruit Salad
(Mixed fresh fruits, chocolate and
nuts in fresh yoghurt and cream)   93

Recipes

OLD ENGLISH TRIFLE

Serves 6–8
   8 sponge cakes
   400g (1 lb) raspberry jam
   100g (4 oz) macaroons
   100g (4 oz) ratafia biscuits
   75g (3 oz) chopped almonds
   grated rind of 1 lemon
   150ml (¼ pint) sherry
   1 wineglass brandy
   3 egg yolks
   50g (2 oz) sugar
   good pinch each of cinnamon and grated nutmeg
   600ml (1 pint) milk
   600 ml (1 pint) double cream
   1 teaspoon icing sugar

For Decoration
   crystallized fruit

To Make
1) Split the sponge cakes and spread with jam. Put into a
   large trifle dish in layers with the macaroons, ratafias,
   almonds and lemon rind and pour over the sherry and
   brandy.
2) Beat the egg yolks with the sugar and spices, warm the
   milk and pour slowly onto the egg yolks. Return to
   the pan and cook gently until thick, stirring all the

time. Pour over the sponges and biscuits. Allow to
cool.

To Serve
Whip the cream and icing sugar together until thick. Pile
on top of the trifle and decorate with crystallized fruits.

BAKED EGGS

Serves 6
   25g (1 oz) butter
   2 rashers bacon, derinded and chopped
   1 small onion, chopped
   2 tomatoes, skinned, seeded and chopped
   1 teaspoon chopped parsley
   6 large eggs
   150 ml (¼ pint) double cream
   salt and freshly ground black pepper

For Garnish
   sprigs of fresh parsley

To Cook
1) Melt the butter in a small pan and fry the bacon and
   onion until lightly browned.
2) Add the tomatoes and parsley and cook for a further 2
   minutes. Season lightly.
3) Divide the bacon mixture and spread evenly in the
   bottom of six ramekins. Crack an egg into each then
   spoon over a little cream. Season to taste.
4) Bake for 6–8 minutes at 190°C (375°F) Gas Mark 5; the
   egg whites should be just set and the yolks runny.

To Serve
Serve straight from the oven in the ramekins. Decorate
each with a sprig of fresh parsley.

BEEF IN RED WINE WITH MUSHROOMS*

Serves 6
  50g (2 oz) beef dripping
  800g (2 lb) lean chuck steak cut into 5cm (2in) chunks
  bouquet garni
  1 clove garlic
  50g (2 oz) carrots   } finely chopped
  50g (2 oz) onions
  25g (1 oz) plain flour
  300ml (½ pint) red wine
  300ml (½ pint) beef stock
  ½ teaspoon thyme
  salt and freshly ground black pepper
  400g (1 lb) small white onions, about 2.5cm (1in) in
    diameter, peeled but left whole
  200g (½ lb) button mushrooms, wiped clean
  50g (2 oz) butter

For Garnish
freshly chopped parsley

To Cook
1) Melt the dripping in a large pan. Brown the cubes of
   meat a few at a time, adding more dripping if necessary;
   transfer to a large oven-proof casserole dish. Bury the
   bouquet garni in the meat.
2) When all the meat is browned fry the chopped garlic,
   carrots and onions for 1–2 minutes. Stir in the flour
   then slowly add the wine and beef stock, whisking
   well as the sauce comes to the boil.
3) Add the thyme, season and pour over the meat. Place
   in the oven at 180°C (350°F) Gas Mark 4 and cook for
   2–3 hours, until the meat is very tender.
4) While the meat cooks, prepare the small white onions
   and the mushrooms. Melt 25 g (1 oz) of the butter in a

frying pan and brown the onions on all sides. Put into an oven-proof dish and place in the oven to bake for 30 minutes. Set on one side.

5) Melt the remaining butter in a frying pan and cook the mushrooms gently for 3 minutes. Add to the onions. Fifteen minutes before the end of cooking time for the meat, stir the onions and mushrooms into the casserole and return it to the oven to finish cooking.

To Serve

Serve straight from the casserole, sprinkled with fresh parsley.

GREEN FRUIT SALAD

Serves 6
100g (4 oz) caster sugar
150ml (¼ pint) water
juice of ½ lemon
2 green apples
2 kiwi fruit
200g (8oz) green grapes
½ small melon

To Make

1) Make the syrup by melting the sugar in the water and lemon juice over a low heat then simmering for 2 minutes.

2) Prepare the fruits: seed, core, peel and cut into small pieces. Put into a pretty serving dish, pour over the syrup and chill for 2–3 hours.

POTTED SHRIMPS

Serves 6
100g (4 oz) butter
400g (1 lb) peeled shrimps

cayenne pepper
mace
salt
50g (2 oz) clarified butter★ (approx)

To Cook

1) Melt the butter over a gentle heat. Stir in the shrimps and season with cayenne, mace and salt to taste.
2) Heat through but do not allow to boil. Transfer to small ramekins and pour over the clarified butter. Chill.

To Serve

Allow one ramekin per person and serve with lots of hot toast.

★To clarify butter, melt it gently until the small solids separate from the fat. Pass through a piece of muslin to strain thoroughly. The clarified butter is now ready for use or can be stored in the fridge until needed.

CROWN ROAST OF LAMB

Serves 6–7

1 prepared Crown Roast of Lamb (most good butchers will do this to order)
mint and rosemary stuffing, see page 56 (optional)
1 onion, peeled but whole
300ml (½ pint) stock
1 tablespoon plain flour
1 tablespoon mint jelly
salt and freshly ground black pepper

For Garnish

cutlet frills

To Cook

1) Fill the crown with the stuffing (if using) and set in a roasting tray with the whole onion. Pour in 2 table-spoons of stock.
2) Place in the preheated oven at 180°C (350°F) Gas Mark 4 and roast for 25–35 minutes per lb. When cooked, take up the crown and carefully transfer to a serving plate. Keep warm whilst you finish the gravy. A stuffed crown roast will need the longer cooking time.
3) Discard the onion and pour off most of the fat from the roasting tin.
4) Stir in the flour and add the stock and mint jelly. Bring to the boil, simmer for 5 minutes, season and serve in a gravy boat.

To Serve

Decorate the crown with the cutlet frills. If you have not stuffed the crown roast use the rice and peas mixed together to fill the crown. Carve at the table by cutting down each cutlet.

BAKED RICE

Serves 6 as a vegetable
   50g (2 oz) butter
   1 onion, finely chopped
   200g (8 oz) long grain rice
   900 ml (1½ pints) stock
   salt and freshly ground black pepper

To Cook

1) Melt the butter in a large pan and fry the onion until soft but not browned.
2) Add the rice and stir well to coat each grain with the

butter. Add the stock, season, bring to the boil and
pour into an oven-proof casserole dish.
3) Bake at 190°C (375°F) Gas Mark 5 for 20–30 minutes,
until the stock is absorbed.

STRAWBERRY PAVLOVA

Serves 6–8
　4 egg whites
　200g (8 oz) caster sugar
　1 teaspoon cornflour
　½ teaspoon vinegar
　3–4 drops vanilla essence
　300 ml (½ pint) double cream, whipped
　400g (1 lb) fresh strawberries, halved

To Cook
1) Whisk the egg whites until stiff. Fold in the sugar a
spoonful at a time; continue whisking until the mixture
is very stiff. Beat in the cornflour, vinegar and vanilla
essence.
2) Pipe or spoon the mixture onto a baking sheet covered
with non-stick baking paper, smoothing into a round
shape, and bake at 140°C (275°F) Gas Mark 1 for 1–2
hours, until crisp and dry.

To Serve
One hour before serving fill the case with the whipped
cream. Arrange the strawberry halves in neat circles on
top of the cream.

N.B. There are so many different possible toppings it's
impossible to list them but our favourite variations are:
kiwi fruit and fresh pineapple arranged in separate circles;

raspberries with freshly poached pears; and strawberries either on their own or with a kiwi fruit circle for contrast.

HOT STUFFED TOMATOES

Serves 6
   6 large tomatoes
   25g (1 oz) butter
   2 rashers bacon, derinded and chopped
   1 small onion
   1 small green pepper } chopped
   1 tablespoon chopped parsley
   50g (2 oz) fresh breadcrumbs
   25g (1 oz) Parmesan cheese, grated
   salt and freshly ground black pepper

For Garnish
   sprigs of fresh parsley

To Cook
1) Slice off the tops of the tomatoes and reserve. Scoop out the pulp with a teaspoon. Turn the tomatoes upside down and leave to drain.
2) Melt the butter in a frying pan and fry the bacon, onion and pepper until soft and lightly coloured. Remove from the heat.
3) Stir in the parsley, breadcrumbs, cheese and tomato pulp. Season to taste.
4) Spoon this mixture into the tomato shells and put back their 'lids'. Bake for 20 minutes at 180°C (350°F) Gas Mark 4.

To Serve
Gently *slide* a tomato onto a small plate. Pop a sprig of fresh parsley under the 'lid' and serve at once.

ROAST LOIN OF PORK DIJONNAIS

Serves 6
1 tablespoon Dijon mustard
1 tablespoon soft brown sugar
3 tablespoons fresh brown breadcrumbs
1 wineglass white wine
1½kg (3 lb) loin of pork, chined
8 cloves
25g (1 oz) butter
1 small onion, chopped
1 tablespoon flour
300 ml (½ pint) stock
1 teaspoon tomato purée
salt and freshly ground black pepper

To Cook
1) Mix the mustard, sugar and breadcrumbs together with 1 tablespoon of the wine.
2) Trim the rind from the pork and spread the mixture evenly over the fat. Stud with the cloves.
3) Put the pork into a roasting tin with one tablespoon water and roast at 190°C (375°F) Gas Mark 5 for 25 minutes per lb plus 25 minutes over.
4) Melt the butter in a frying pan and cook the onion until soft and brown. Stir in the flour, cook gently until browned. Pour over the stock, the remaining wine and the tomato purée. Stir well, season and simmer for 5 minutes. Set aside.
5) When the meat has finished cooking put onto a serving plate and keep warm.
6) Pour off the fat from the roasting tin, add the sauce to the remaining juices and blend well over a gentle heat. Check seasoning.

To Serve
Carve the meat from the bone; because of the chining the meat should come away easily. Carve into 0.5cm (¼in)

thick slices, arrange on a warmed serving platter and mask with a little of the sauce. Serve the rest of the sauce separately in a sauceboat.

BOULANGERE POTATOES

Serves 6
- 800g (2 lb) potatoes, peeled and sliced 0.5cm (¼in) thick
- 800g (2 lb) onions, sliced
- salt and freshly ground black pepper
- 600ml (1 pint) stock

To Cook
1) Arrange the potato and onion slices in an oven-proof casserole dish, seasoning each layer lightly.
2) Pour over the stock and bake for 1½–2 hours at 180°C (350°F) Gas Mark 4 until cooked through and golden brown.

To Serve
Serve straight from the dish they were cooked in.

MARIANNE'S FRUIT SALAD

Serves 6
- 2 apples, peeled, cored and chopped
- 2 satsumas, peeled and pulled into segments
- ½ melon, seeded, peeled and chopped
- 50g (2 oz) grapes, seeded and halved
- 25g (1 oz) dark chocolate, grated
- 25g (1 oz) walnuts, chopped
- 150ml (¼ pint) natural yoghurt
- 150ml (¼ pint) fresh cream

1 tablespoon caster sugar
2–3 drops almond essence

To Make

1) Combine the fruits, chocolate and nuts in a large bowl.
2) Mix together the yoghurt, cream, sugar and almond essence.
3) Pour the cream mixture over the fruit and gently fold to mix.

To Serve

Put into a pretty serving dish. Decorate with whole nuts, grated chocolate, fruit or whatever takes your fancy!

Timetables

These timetables are worked out to give an 8.00 p.m. sitting-down time. Again, adjustments can be made lightly in pencil and erased later.

TIMETABLE FOR MENU NO. 12

Baked Eggs

. . .

Beef in Red Wine with Mushrooms
Creamed Potatoes

. . .

Green Fruit Salad

2–3 Weeks Ahead
Make up Beef in Red Wine and freeze.

During the Morning
Make up Beef in Red Wine (if not frozen). Take from freezer if frozen.
Prepare fruit salad and refrigerate.
Peel potatoes.
Make and cook bacon mixture and put into bottom of ramekins.

Start Time .... p.m.
Place the beef in the oven (if not frozen).

To Finish Cooking
7.00 p.m. Put beef into oven to warm through.
7.15 p.m. Boil potatoes in lightly salted water.

7.45 p.m.   Crack eggs into ramekins, add cream and
            bake 6–8 minutes.
7.50 p.m.   Take fruit salad from fridge to 'come to'.
            Mash potatoes, keep warm.
8.00 p.m.   Serve first course.

TIMETABLE FOR MENU NO. 13

Potted Shrimps
                    . . .
Crown Roast of Lamb, Baked Rice, Peas,
New Potatoes, Glazed Carrots
                    . . .
Fresh Strawberry Pavlova

During the Morning
Pot shrimps.
Prepare vegetables.
Make Pavlova.

Start Time .... p.m.
Put lamb in oven.

To Finish Cooking
7.00 p.m.   Put carrots and rice into oven.
            Fill Pavlova.
7.30 p.m.   Put on potatoes to boil.
7.40 p.m.   Take out meat, set to keep warm. Make
            gravy, simmer.
            Put plates to warm.
7.50 p.m.   Cook peas, drain and mix with rice. Keep
            warm.
7.55 p.m.   Make toast.
8.00 p.m.   Serve shrimps.

TIMETABLE FOR MENU NO. 14

Hot Stuffed Tomatoes
   . . .

Roast Loin of Pork Dijonnais
Boulangère Potatoes, Brussels Sprouts
with Nuts
   . . .

Marianne's Fruit Salad

During the Morning
Make filling and stuff tomatoes.
Prepare and coat meat.
Make up sauce base.
Assemble boulangère potatoes (make sure the stock covers them so they don't go brown).
Prepare sprouts.
Make and refrigerate fruit salad.

Start Time .... p.m.
Put meat and potatoes into oven.

To Finish Cooking
7.40 p.m.   Put tomatoes into oven.
             Take out pork and make sauce. Put plates to warm.
7.50 p.m.   Take fruit salad from fridge.
             Cook sprouts for 5–6 minutes, drain and keep warm.
8.00 p.m.   Serve tomatoes. Mix sprouts with salted almonds before serving main course.

'The Day After'

The 'eating-up' day should be enjoyable. The following recipes have been carefully chosen and are suitable for either turkey or 'Big Chicken'.

Using different herbs or spices will help to make meals where no-one mutters 'left-overs'

Choose from:

The ham is perhaps best sliced for sandwiches, but why not ring the changes with a delicious Croque Monsieur or

Madame (page 106) for a light lunch, or a more exotic
'Nasi Goreng' (page 107).

Recipes

TURKEY PIE WITH PEPPERS AND CHEESE

Serves 4–6
   50g (2 oz) butter
   1 onion, chopped
   2 red peppers, seeded and chopped
   50g (2 oz) plain flour
   600ml (1 pint) chicken or turkey stock
   100g (4 oz) Cheddar cheese
   400g (1 lb) cooked turkey, diced
   salt and freshly ground black pepper
   325g (13 oz) puff pastry (frozen is suitable)
   1 egg, beaten

To Cook
1) Melt the butter in a large pan and fry the onion and peppers until soft but not brown.
2) Stir in the flour and cook for 2 minutes. Do not allow to brown. Add the stock, bring slowly to the boil, whisking all the time. Simmer for 2 minutes.
3) Add the cheese and turkey, season, mix gently and pour into a 1.8 litre (3 pint) pie dish.
4) Roll out the pastry and cover the pie. Glaze with the egg and decorate.
5) Bake for 20 minutes at 240°C (450°F) Gas Mark 8 then turn the heat down to 160°C (325°F) Gas Mark 3 and bake for a further 40 minutes.

To Serve
Serve straight from the oven. The mixture isn't at all dry so nothing else will be needed other than a few boiled or creamed potatoes and perhaps a green vegetable.

TURKEY RISOTTO

Serves 4–6
  25g (1 oz) butter
  2 rashers bacon, derinded and chopped
  1 large onion, chopped
  1 green pepper, seeded and chopped
  100g (4 oz) mushrooms, wiped clean and sliced
  200g (8 oz) turkey, diced
  200g (8 oz) long grain rice
  750ml (1¼ pint) chicken or turkey stock
  salt and freshly ground black pepper

To Cook
1) Melt the butter in a large pan and fry the bacon, onion and pepper until soft and lightly coloured.
2) Add the mushrooms, turkey and rice, pour over the stock and season.
3) Pour into an oven-proof casserole dish and bake at 160°C (325°F) Gas Mark 3 for 35 minutes, until the rice has absorbed the stock.

To Serve
Fluff-up the rice lightly and serve straight from the cook-ing pot.

TURKEY CHILLI

Serves 4–6
  2 tablespoons olive oil
  1 onion, chopped
  1 green pepper, seeded and chopped
  1 small green chilli, seeded and chopped
  1 stick of celery, chopped
  1 clove of garlic, chopped

1 tablespoon plain flour
300ml (½ pint) turkey or chicken stock
400g (1 lb) cooked turkey, diced
salt
cayenne pepper
chilli powder

To Cook

1) Heat the oil in a large heavy pan and fry the onion, pepper, chilli, celery and garlic until soft but not brown.
2) Stir in the flour then pour over the stock.
3) Mix in the diced turkey, season with salt and cayenne pepper and simmer for 10–15 minutes.
4) Check the seasoning, adding a little chilli powder if needed.

To Serve

Serve with a large baked potato per person and perhaps a salad dressed with natural yoghurt. Cooked red kidney beans can be added if preferred.

TURKEY PASTIES

Serves 4–6
25g (1 oz) butter
50g (2 oz) onion, finely chopped
50g (2 oz) green pepper, finely chopped
200g (8 oz) cooked turkey, diced small
1 tablespoon freshly chopped parsley
2 tablespoons stock or turkey gravy
salt and freshly ground black pepper
200g (8oz) pastry (see Basic Preparations, page 151)
1 egg, beaten

To Cook

1) Melt the butter in a frying pan and cook the onion and pepper until soft but not coloured. Stir in the turkey, parsley and stock or gravy and season. Remove from the heat.
2) Roll out the pastry and cut into 10cm (4in) squares or circles. Put a little filling on each piece of pastry and fold over, sealing with the beaten egg. Glaze the pasties with the remaining egg and decorate to taste.
3) Place on a baking sheet and bake at 190°C (375°F) Gas Mark 4 for 15 minutes, until golden brown.

To Serve

The pasties make a pleasant light meal just served warm from the oven with a salad.

CROQUE MONSIEUR

Serves 6

150g (6 oz) Gruyère cheese, thinly sliced
6 slices cooked ham (lean)
12 slices bread cut 1cm (½in) thick
sewing thread
100g (4 oz) butter

To Cook

1) Cover 6 slices of the bread firstly with ham then with cheese. Top with the remaining 6 slices of bread and tie each sandwich into a parcel with the cotton.
2) Melt the butter in a frying pan. Sauté the parcels on each side until golden brown.

To Serve

Snip off the cotton and serve at once.

N.B. To do a Croque Madame, follow the same recipe but serve topped with a fried egg.

NASI GORENG

Serves 6
   50g (2 oz) butter
   1 large onion
   1 clove garlic } chopped
   small piece of chilli, seeds removed
   1 tablespoon soy sauce
   ½ teaspoon ground coriander
   1 teaspoon curry powder
   200g (8 oz) cooked rice
   600g (1½ lb) cold roast turkey, or ham or pork (cubed)
   200g (8 oz) cooked peas

For Garnish
   2 eggs, beaten with 1 tablespoon water
   tomato wedges

To Cook
1) Melt the butter and fry the onion and garlic until soft but not coloured.
2) Add the spices and cook for 2 minutes. Add the rice and meat, mix well and when heated stir in the peas.
3) In a frying pan cook the thin omelette mixture gently until set. Cut into strips.

To Serve
Heap the rice mixture into a serving platter. Decorate with a lattice of the egg strips and set the tomato wedges around the edges.

New Year's Eve

For the traditional party evening, here are suggestions for a light meal or snack to keep the hunger-pangs at bay if you are off to a party, or menus for the rather more sophisticated New Year Dinner Parties.

MENU 15: Light Suppers

	page
Creamy Onion Soup	114

· · ·

Country-style Pâté★	114
or	
Bacon and Egg Mille Feuilles	115
or	
Coulibiac with Cabbage Filling	116
or	
Hot Pot	117

END OF YEAR DINNER PARTIES

MENU 16: 'Sophisticats' Dinner Party
(See Timetable, page 125)

	page
Terrine of Plaice and Smoked Salmon	118

· · ·

Roast Duck Breasts in Green

Party Time

Peppercorn Sauce, Potato Balls,
Matchstick Carrots and Parsnips   119–21

. . .

Pear, Almond and Brandy Tart   121

MENU 17: Light Gamey Dinner Party
(See Timetable, page 126)

page

Tomato Sorbet★ with Avocado   122

. . .

Recipes

CREAMY ONION SOUP

Serves 4–6
    50g (2 oz) butter
    800g (2 lb) onions, finely chopped
    1.2 litres (2 pints) milk
    grated nutmeg
    salt and freshly ground black pepper
    150ml (¼ pint) double cream

To Cook
1) Melt the butter in a large heavy pan, add the onions, cover and cook until soft but not coloured.
2) Pour over the milk, grate over some nutmeg and season with salt and pepper.
3) Simmer gently for 30 minutes. Stir in the cream and taste for seasoning and nutmeg.

To Serve
Serve in a warmed tureen or large pot. Ladle into soup bowls at the table.

COUNTRY-STYLE PATE*

Serves 6
    3–4 rashers streaky bacon
    50g (2 oz) bread
    1 tablespoon port
    200g (8 oz) pork, minced coarsely

100g (4 oz) pig's liver, minced coarsely
50g (2 oz) onion, finely chopped
1 teaspoon mixed herbs
good pinch allspice
salt and freshly ground black pepper
2 eggs, beaten

For Garnish
pickled gherkins

To Cook
1) Line a loaf tin with the streaky bacon, cutting to size where necessary. Prepare the water jacket by pouring warm water into the base of a large roasting tin. The water should come two-thirds of the way up the loaf tin containing the pâté.
2) Soak the bread with the port. Mix together with all the remaining dry ingredients and bind with the egg. Taste for seasoning by frying a small piece of the mixture.
3) Turn the mixture into the loaf tin. Smooth down and cover with foil.
4) Cook in a water jacket at 180°C (350°F) Gas Mark 4 for 1½ hours. Take off the foil. Cover the loaf with greaseproof paper and press lightly until cold.

To Serve
Cut into neat slices; the bacon surround looks most effective this way. Pickled gherkins are excellent with this pâté, but toast is not essential since it isn't very rich.

BACON AND EGG MILLE FEUILLES

Serves 4
370g (13 oz) puff pastry (frozen is most suitable)
50g (2 oz) butter

50g (2 oz) onion, chopped
50g (2 oz) red pepper, chopped
100g (4 oz) bacon, derinded and chopped
6 eggs, beaten
salt and freshly ground black pepper

For Garnish
2 tomatoes, sliced downwards

To Cook
1) Divide the pastry into three. Roll out into rectangles measuring 30 × 15cm (12 × 6in). Place on a baking sheet and bake for 12–15 minutes at 200°C (400°F) Gas Mark 6, until golden brown. Melt 25g (1 oz) of the butter in a frying pan and fry the pepper and onion until soft but not coloured.
2) Grill the bacon pieces and keep warm.
3) Melt the remaining butter, season the eggs and scramble them in the butter until they form soft curds. Stir in the bacon, pepper and onion.

To Serve
Sandwich the egg mixture between the pastry pieces and serve at once, garnishing with the sliced tomatoes.

COULIBIAC WITH CABBAGE FILLING

Serves 6
1.25kg (3 lb) white cabbage, shredded
100g (4 oz) butter
200g (8 oz) onions, chopped
4 hard-boiled eggs, chopped
1 teaspoon dried dill *or* 2 teaspoon chopped fresh dill
salt and freshly ground black pepper

500g (20 oz) puff pastry (frozen is fine)
1 egg, beaten

For Garnish
watercress or fresh parsley sprigs

To Cook
1) Cook the cabbage in boiling salted water for 5 minutes. Drain well.
2) Melt 50g (2 oz) of the butter in a large pan and fry the onion until soft but not brown. Add the cabbage and cover, pushing down lightly, and simmer very gently for 30 minutes. Drain and mix with the chopped eggs, herbs and seasoning.
3) Take two-thirds of the pastry and roll out to a rectangle. Place on a greased baking sheet.
4) Heap the cabbage filling onto the pastry.
5) Roll out the remaining pastry, put over the filling and seal by rolling the bottom pastry edge upwards over the top piece of pastry. Crimp, decorate and glaze with the beaten egg. (The finished coulibiac should have the shape of an elongated oval). Snip an air hole in the top to let out the steam during cooking.
6) Bake at 200°C (400°F) Gas Mark 6 for about 1 hour.

To Serve
Melt the remaining butter and pour into the coulibiac via the air hole just before serving. Serve decorated with watercress or parsley and carve at the table.

HOT POT

Serves 4–6
800g (2 lb) potatoes
400g (1 lb) onions

salt and freshly ground black pepper
600ml (1 pint) stock
6 lamb cutlets or neck chops, trimmed of fat

To Cook

1) Peel the potatoes and slice about 0.5cm (¼in) thick. Peel and slice the onions into rings.
2) Arrange the potatoes and onions in an oven-proof casserole in alternate rings, season well and pour over the stock. Cook, covered, for 30–40 minutes at 180°C (350°F) Gas Mark 4.
3) Remove from the oven, take off the lid and arrange the lamb chops on top of the vegetables. Put back into the oven to cook for a further 60 minutes, turning the chops once.

To Serve

Blot any excess fat from the top of the casserole with dry bread or kitchen paper and serve straight from the cooking pot. The best accompaniment for hot pot is pickled red cabbage.

TERRINE OF PLAICE AND SMOKED SALMON

Serves 4–6
400g (1 lb) plaice fillets, skinned, boned and chopped
salt, grated nutmeg and cayenne pepper
2 egg whites, whisked until stiff
300ml (½ pint) double cream
200g (½ lb) smoked salmon, thinly sliced

For Garnish

lemon wedges and watercress

To Cook
1) Pound the plaice to a smooth purée, using either a mortar or food processor.
2) Season with salt, nutmeg and cayenne pepper then beat in the egg whites a little at a time. Add the cream and continue to beat until smooth. Prepare a water jacket by pouring warm water into a large roasting tin. The water needs to come two-thirds of the way up the loaf tin when the terrine is cooking.
3) Line a loaf tin with buttered greaseproof paper then cover the bottom and sides with about two-thirds of the smoked salmon.
4) Pour in half the plaice mixture, put in a layer of smoked salmon, followed by the rest of the mousse. Cover with buttered greaseproof paper and bake in a water jacket at 180°C (350°F) Gas Mark 4 for 1 hour.
5) Allow to cool in the tin.

To Serve
Cut into slices and garnish with a lemon wedge and some watercress.

ROAST DUCK BREASTS IN GREEN PEPPERCORN SAUCE

Serves 4
  4 breast portions of duck 'on the bone'
  salt and freshly ground black pepper
  1 tablespoon olive oil
  150ml (¼ pint) dry white wine
  2 tablespoons cognac
  150ml (¼ pint) chicken stock
  300ml (½ pint) double cream
  1 tablespoon wine vinegar
  1 scant teaspoon caster sugar

1 tablespoon port
25g (1 oz) sweet red pepper, diced small
25g (1 oz) green peppercorns

For Garnish
watercress

To Cook
1) Season the duck breasts with salt and freshly ground black pepper; put into an oven-proof dish, meat side down. Sprinkle with olive oil and cook for 20 minutes at 240°C (475°F) Gas Mark 9.
2) Turn the oven heat down to 150°C (300°F) Gas Mark 2 and cover the dish with foil.
3) Boil the wine and cognac until reduced by two-thirds. Add the stock and simmer until reduced by one-third.
4) In another small pan bring the vinegar and sugar to the boil and cook until they caramelize. This usually forms just a brown covering on the bottom of the pan. Pour in the sauce, cream and port stirring well, then add the diced peppers and peppercorns. Check seasoning and keep warm.

To Serve
Ease the breast meat away from the duck bones. Skin and slice each fillet across the width into medallion shapes. Serve 'fanned' out on the plate, masked with a little of the sauce and garnished with watercress.

POTATO BALLS

Serves 4
400g (1 lb) potatoes, peeled
1 egg, separated
4 tablespoons chopped parsley

50g (2 oz) fresh white breadcrumbs
50g (2 oz) butter

To Cook

1) Boil the potatoes in lightly salted water. Drain and mash, using the egg yolk to moisten. Beat in the parsley and season.
2) Whisk the egg white until frothy.
3) Shape the potato mixture into balls about 4cm (1½in) in diameter and coat with the egg whites, then roll in the breadcrumbs. Repeat until well covered.
4) Melt the butter in an oven-proof dish, put in the potato balls and turn to coat with the butter.
5) Bake for 1 hour at 180°C (350°F) Gas Mark 6 until crisp and brown.

To Serve

Serve straight from the oven, whilst they are crisp.

PEAR, ALMOND AND BRANDY TART

Serves 4–6

200g (8 oz) caster sugar
150g (6 oz) ground almonds
½ teaspoon cinnamon
800g (2 lb) pears, peeled, cored and quartered
50g (2 oz) butter
3 tablespoons brandy
370g (13oz) puff pastry (frozen is fine)
1 egg, beaten

To Cook

1) Mix together the sugar, almonds and cinnamon.
2) Arrange the pears in a shallow pie dish. Dot with butter and sprinkle with brandy.

3) Pour the sugar mixture over the pears and smooth down.
4) Roll out the pastry, cover the pie and decorate to taste. Glaze with the beaten egg.
5) Bake for 15 minutes at 220°C (425°F) Gas Mark 7 then reduce the oven heat to 190°C (375°F) Gas Mark 5, and bake for a further 25 minutes, until the pastry is golden brown.

To Serve
Serve warm or cold, with cream if liked.

TOMATO SORBET* WITH AVOCADO

Serves 4
   400g (1 lb) ripe tomatoes
   1 teaspoon tomato purée
   ½ teaspoon chopped fresh parsley
   pinch of sugar
   salt and freshly ground black pepper
   150 ml (¼ pint) double cream
   2 large ripe avocados

To Make
1) Peel the tomatoes by first covering them with boiling water, leave for 1 minute then plunge into cold water after which the skins can be easily removed. Discard the seeds and chop the tomato flesh coarsely.
2) Mash the tomatoes either by using a liquidizer or pushing them through a sieve. Mix in a teaspoon of tomato purée and the parsley and sugar. Season lightly.
3) Beat the cream until stiff and fold into the tomato mixture. Turn into a freezer container and freeze until just before needed. (The flavour develops more when

frozen so don't worry if the mixture tastes a little bland now).

4) Cut the avocados in half, remove the stones and the skins. Slice thinly lengthwise.

To Serve

Arrange the avocado portions on a plate in a fan or wheel shape, with a scoop of tomato sorbet in the centre.

PHEASANT WITH SOURED CREAM

Serves 4

    50 g (2 oz) butter
    2 pheasants, cleaned and oven ready
    6 shallots or spring onions, chopped
    300ml (½ pint) white wine
    1 level tablespoon flour
    150ml (¼ pint) soured cream
    salt and freshly ground black pepper

For Garnish

    watercress

To Cook

1) Melt the butter in a large heavy pan. Add the birds and slowly brown on all sides.
2) Add 1 tablespoon of shallots (or spring onions) and 2 tablespoons of white wine, season, cover and cook gently for 30–40 minutes on top of the stove, turning the birds once or twice as they cook.
3) In another pan, boil the remaining wine and shallots together and reduce by half.
4) When the birds are cooked, take from the pan and set aside, covered, to keep warm.
5) Pour off the fat from the cooking pan, stir the flour

into the remaining juices, add the wine and shallot mixture and simmer for 2 minutes. Strain, put back into the pan and add the cream. Simmer until thick and creamy. Check seasoning.

To Serve
Carve the pheasants, arrange on a serving dish and pour over the sauce. Put bunches of watercress at each end of the dish.

ORANGES IN CARAMEL

Serves 4
300 ml (½ pint) water
200g (8 oz) sugar
4 oranges (seedless if possible)

For Garnish
blanched orange peel parings (optional)

To Cook
1) Put half the water and all the sugar into a pan and boil until the mixture caramelizes. Carefully add the rest of the water, cover and set aside.
2) Peel the oranges, remove all the pith, slice into rounds and remove any seeds.
3) Re-shape into oranges and secure with cocktail sticks.
4) Put the oranges into a deep dish and pour over the caramel. Chill well.

To Serve
Serve straight from the fridge decorated if wished with thin parings of orange peel that have been blanched.

TIMETABLE FOR MENU NO. 16

Terrine of Plaice and Smoked Salmon

. . .

Duck Breasts with Peppercorn Sauce
Potato Balls, Matchstick Carrots and
Parsnips

. . .

Pear, Almond and Brandy Tart

During the Morning

Make up terrine and refrigerate.
Make up tart, bake.
Prepare potato balls to final cooking stage.
Prepare vegetables.

Start Time .... p.m.

To Finish Cooking

7.00 p.m.   Put potato balls in oven.
7.30 p.m.   Turn oven up for duck, move potato balls to
            oven floor.
            Take terrine from fridge.
7.35 p.m.   Put duck portions in oven.
7.40 p.m.   Start to make sauce.
            Put plates to warm.
7.55 p.m.   Turn oven down – cover duck with foil.
            Put vegetables on – cook for 5 minutes, drain
            and keep warm.
8.00 p.m.   Serve the terrine. Put the tart to re-heat.

Finish the sauce and carve the duck just before serving. Toss the vegetables in butter.

TIMETABLE FOR MENU NO. 17

Tomato Sorbet with Avocado

. . .

Pheasant with Soured Cream
Duchesse Potatoes, Haricots Verts

. . .

Oranges in Caramel

The Day Before
Make up and freeze sorbet.

During the Morning
Make caramel and prepare oranges, refrigerate.
Make up base for sauce for pheasants by boiling wine and shallots until reduced by half. (Remember to keep 2 tablespoons of wine and 1 tablespoon of shallots on one side to add to the pheasants).
Boil, mash and pipe potatoes on to a baking sheet.
Trim beans.

Start Time .... p.m.

To Finish Cooking
7.00 p.m.   Start to cook pheasants.
7.30 p.m.   Put potatoes in oven.
              Take sorbet from freezer.
7.50 p.m.   Finish pheasant sauce. Keep warm.
              Put on beans to cook. Put plates to warm.
7.55 p.m.   Peel and prepare avocados.

8.00 p.m.   Drain beans and keep warm.
Serve avocado and sorbet.
Carve the pheasants and pour over the sauce
just before serving.

New Year's Day

The first day of the New Year seems tailor-made for the most traditional of roasts. What better way to start the New Year than with the 'Traditional Roast Ribs of Beef' menu? It has Yorkshire puddings, horseradish sauce, roast potatoes – everything, in fact, that has become traditionally associated with the most popular of all British meals.

But perhaps the 'Celebration Roast Leg of Pork' would fit in better with your other menu plans. It is every bit as traditional, with apple sauce and sage and onion stuffing balls to complement the meat, and any left-overs can be made into a really delicious 'Nasi Goreng' on the 2nd. The syrup pudding is incredibly light and has a lovely flavour.

Our final menu suggestion has a whole fresh salmon or sea trout main course, served with a freshly made hollandaise sauce (don't worry, this sauce is so *easy* to make!). It is a wonderful first menu for any year and looks truly magnificent!

MENU 18: **Traditional Roast Ribs of Beef**
(See Timetable, page 143)

page

Homemade Creamy Mushroom
Soup   131

. . .

Roast Ribs of Beef, Yorkshire
Puddings, Horseradish Sauce, Roast
Potatoes, Parsnips and Onions,

MENU 19: Celebration Roast Leg of Pork
(See Timetable, page 144)

MENU 20: Magnificent Whole Fresh Salmon
(See Timetable, page 145)

Recipes

HOMEMADE CREAMY MUSHROOM SOUP

Serves 6
    25g (1 oz) butter
    200g (½ lb) flat mushrooms, wiped clean and sliced
    2 onions, chopped
    2 tablespoons flour
    300ml (½ pint) chicken stock
    900ml (1½ pints) milk
    salt and freshly ground black pepper

To Cook
1) Melt the butter in a large pan, add the mushrooms and onions, cover and cook gently until soft.
2) Stir in the flour, pour over the chicken stock and milk, season and simmer gently for 15–20 minutes.

To Serve
Check seasoning, and pour into a warmed tureen or large bowl. Ladle into soup plates at the table.

ROAST RIBS OF BEEF

    2kg (5 lb) sirloin of beef, chined
    1 onion, peeled but left whole
    salt and freshly ground black pepper
    1 tablespoon flour
    300ml (½ pint) beef stock

To Cook

1) Put the beef and onion into a roasting tin, sprinkle with black pepper all over and salt just on the fat.
2) Roast, uncovered, for 15 minutes at 220°C (425°F) Gas Mark 7 then lower the oven heat to 190°C (375°F) Gas Mark 5 for the rest of the cooking time. Allow 15 minutes per lb for rare meat, 20 minutes per lb for medium. Add an extra 15 minutes for resting time.
3) When the meat has finished cooking, take from the roasting tin and keep warm. Pour off the excess fat from the tin and stir in the flour. Add the stock and simmer for 5 minutes. Check for seasoning.

To Serve

Carve the beef and arrange on a platter surrounded with small Yorkshire puddings and roast potatoes. Alternatively, take the joint to the table and carve there. Either way, hand the gravy separately in a sauceboat.

HORSERADISH SAUCE

50g (2 oz) horseradish root
150ml (¼ pint) double cream
1 teaspoon caster sugar
1 teaspoon white wine vinegar
salt

To Make

1) Scrape the horseradish and soak for 1 hour. Grate coarsely, being careful not to get any juice near your eyes.
2) Whip the cream until stiff, fold in the grated horseradish, sugar and vinegar, check for seasoning and add salt to taste.

To Serve
Turn into a pretty dish and hand separately. Beware, this creamed horseradish is much hotter than the bought variety!

YORKSHIRE PUDDINGS

Gives 12 small puddings
   100g (4 oz) plain flour
   ½ teaspoon salt
   2 eggs
   300ml (½ pint) milk
   1 tablespoon cold water
   dripping

To Cook
1) Sieve the flour and salt into a bowl, crack in the eggs and pour in half the milk.
2) Beat gently at first to blend all ingredients; when smooth add the remaining milk and the water and beat well. Leave to stand for at least half an hour in a cool place.
3) Using a bun tin, put a little dripping into each section and place in the oven. When the fat is smoking pour in the batter. Cook for 15–20 minutes at 200°C (400°F) Gas Mark 6 until brown and crisp.

To Serve
These small Yorkshire Puddings look lovely surrounding the meat but they must be served straight from the oven to keep them crisp. (My first mother-in-law thought these 'Yorkshires' were best served with sugar sprinkled on them as a sweet, but then she always took her dumplings from a stew and had them later with syrup poured over.

If your tastes are similar feel free, I'm sure it must be delicious!).

APPLE PIE* AND CHEESE

Serves 6
  300g (12 oz) shortcrust pastry (see Basic Preparations, page 151)
  600g (1½ lb) Bramley apples
  25–50g (1–2 oz) sugar
  2 cloves
  pinch of cinnamon
  1 egg, beaten

To Cook
1) Roll out just over half the pastry to cover the bottom of a 24cm (9½in) metal pie plate; do not trim at this stage.
2) Peel, core and slice the apples, mix with the sugar, cloves and cinnamon. Tip the mixture into the pastry pie base.
3) Roll out the pastry top, cover the pie using the beaten egg to seal and glaze. Trim the edges and flute. Make a hole in the centre of the pie to allow the steam to escape during cooking.
4) Bake for 30 minutes at 200°C (400°F) Gas Mark 6, until golden brown and the pastry is cooked underneath.

To Serve
Serve hot or cold with a wedge of cheese. Wensleydale, Cheshire or Lancashire are most suitable. 'Apple Pie without cheese, is like a kiss without a squeeze', as they say in Yorkshire!

CARROT AND CORIANDER SOUP

Serves 6
   800g (2 lb) carrots
   1.8 litres (3 pints) chicken stock
   1 tablespoon coriander seeds
   ½ teaspoon ground coriander
   salt and freshly ground black pepper

For Garnish
   freshly chopped parsley or coriander

To Cook
1) Scrape the carrots and slice into rounds. Put into a large saucepan with the stock and coriander seeds. Simmer for 1 hour.
2) Either liquidize, mouli or push through a sieve to achieve a smooth texture.
3) Taste for seasoning, adding the ground coriander if necessary. Re-heat gently.

To Serve
Pour the soup into a warmed tureen and sprinkle with a little freshly chopped parsley or coriander if you are fortunate enough to have some.

ROAST LEG OF PORK

   2–3kg (3–6 lb) leg of pork (ask the butcher to remove the pelvic bone for easier carving)
   1–2 tablespoons olive oil
   salt
   1 onion, peeled and left whole
   1 tablespoon flour

To Cook

1) First score the rind with a really sharp knife (a Stanley type is excellent if your husband isn't looking!). Score by doing one central cut then making a herringbone pattern from it.

2) Put the leg onto a rack in a roasting tin and rub the oil well into the skin. Sprinkle well with salt. Put the onion into the bottom of the tin with 2 tablespoons water and place it all into the pre-heated oven, 200°C (400°F) Gas Mark 6, for 10 minutes. Reduce the oven heat to 170°C (325°F) Gas Mark 3 and cook for 25 minutes per lb, basting occasionally.

3) When the meat is cooked take it out of the roasting tin and set to keep warm whilst you finish the gravy.

4) Pour off the fat, discard the onion and stir the flour into the remaining juices. De-glaze the pan with a little water, pour into a saucepan for ease of working and whisk over a low heat until the gravy thickens, adding more water if necessary. Check seasoning and simmer gently for several minutes.

To Serve

First, remove the crackling in two pieces from the central straight score. To carve, use the same technique as for ham – namely, make a cut into the meat at the point where the leg widens on the bone then cut down vertically into it giving a wedge-shape of meat. Carry on cutting down vertically to the bone.

Serve with the crackling, apple sauce, sage and onion balls and gravy handed separately.

SAGE AND ONION BALLS

1 large onion
50g (2 oz) butter

75g (3 oz) fresh brown breadcrumbs
1 tablespoon fresh chopped sage *or*
½ teaspoon dried sage
1 large egg, beaten
salt and freshly ground black pepper
2–3 tablespoons milk

To Cook
1) Peel and chop the onion finely.
2) Melt the butter in a medium-sized pan, add the onion and cook until soft but not coloured.
3) Take from the heat and stir in the breadcrumbs and sage. Season well then add the egg and enough milk to bind the mixture together.
4) Form the stuffing into small balls 2.5cm (1in) in diameter and put onto a greased baking tray.
5) Cook for 30 minutes or so at 170°C (325°F) Gas Mark 3, until light brown and slightly crisp, basting occasionally.

To Serve
Place around the joint with roast potatoes.

LIGHT SYRUP PUDDING

Serves 6
25g (1 oz) butter
2 tablespoons golden syrup
100g (4 oz) wholemeal flour
2½ teaspoons baking powder
2 eggs
100g (4 oz) soft margarine
100g (4 oz) soft brown sugar

To Cook

1) Butter a 900ml (1½ pint) basin well, then put in the syrup.
2) Put all the remaining ingredients into a bowl and beat well until completely blended.
3) Pour this mixture on top of the syrup. Cover loosely with a double layer of buttered foil (shiny side down) and tie with string.
4) Steam for 1½ hours.

To Serve

Take off the foil and turn the pudding onto a warmed plate. Pour over extra syrup if liked and serve with a custard sauce.

SMALL MUSHROOM TARTLETS

Serves 4–6

300g (12 oz) shortcrust pastry (see Basic Preparations, page 151)
1 egg yolk, beaten
400g (1 lb) flat mushrooms
50g (2 oz) butter
25g (1 oz) flour
150ml (¼ pint) chicken stock
6 tablespoons soured cream
salt and freshly ground black pepper
1 tablespoon fresh chopped parsley mixed with chives
1 teaspoon fresh chopped tarragon *or*
½ teaspoon dried tarragon

For Garnish

watercress and lemon wedges

To Cook

1) Roll out the pastry and cut to line 6 small patty tins. Brush with beaten egg yolk and bake for 10–15 minutes at 190°C (375°F) Gas Mark 5, until golden brown. Meanwhile cook the mushrooms.

2) Wipe the mushrooms and slice thinly. Melt three-quarters of the butter in a large pan and cook the mushrooms until soft.

3) In a small pan melt the remaining butter, stir in the flour and cook gently for 2–3 minutes; do not allow to brown. Add the stock and soured cream, whisking well, and cook for a further 2 minutes. Season well and add the herbs.

4) Mix the mushrooms with the sauce.

To Serve

Spoon some of the mixture into each pastry case, decorate with sprigs of watercress and lemon wedges and serve immediately.

WHOLE POACHED SALMON

4–5kg (8–12 lb) salmon, cleaned and gutted
1 onion, sliced
150ml (¼ pint) dry white wine
1 teaspoon mixed herbs
2 slices lemon
10–12 black peppercorns
salt
2 sprigs parsley

For Garnish

lemon wedges, fresh parsley and sliced cucumber

To Cook
1) Make up a court bouillon by gently simmering the onion together with the lemon slices, herbs and seasonings, for 5 minutes.
2) If the salmon is too long for either a large fish kettle or a large shallow roasting tin, take off the head and tail and discard.
3) Put the fish into the kettle or roasting tray, pour over the court bouillon and cover tightly either with the lid or with foil (shiny side down). Using two rings on top of the stove, if necessary, to achieve the most even heat, slowly bring to the boil.
4) Turn the heat down to low and simmer very gently for 10 minutes.
5) Check for 'doneness'; if cooked through, turn off the heat and re-cover tightly to retain the heat whilst you prepare the hollandaise sauce.

To Serve
To prepare the serving dish, decorate with cucumber slices, lemon wedges and parsley sprigs. Remove the skin from the salmon, scraping any grey meat away with it and giving the meaty bits to the cat. Gently ease the salmon onto the centre of the serving plate. Serve the sauce separately.

HOLLANDAISE SAUCE

Serves 6
>   3 large egg yolks
>   1 tablespoon cold water
>   salt and freshly ground black pepper
>   200g (8 oz) butter taken straight from the fridge and cut
>   into small bits
>   1 tablespoon lemon juice

To Cook

1) Use a bain-marie saucepan or make a double pan by using a large saucepan with a trivet in the bottom and a small saucepan on top. Heat some water in the lower pan to simmering point, then turn the heat to low.

2) Put the egg yolks, water and a little salt and pepper into the upper pan and beat until smooth. Add the butter a few pieces at a time and whisk until completely absorbed. When all the butter has been used continue whisking until the sauce becomes thick and creamy. Whisk in the lemon juice and then pour into a warmed sauceboat and serve immediately.

HAZELNUT MERINGUE WITH RASPBERRIES

Serves 6

    4 egg whites
    200g (8 oz) caster sugar
    ½ teaspoon vinegar
    3 drops vanilla essence
    100g (4 oz) roasted chopped hazelnuts
    200g (8 oz) raspberries (fresh or frozen)
    300ml (½ pint) double cream

To Cook

1) Line two sandwich tins with non-stick baking parchment.

2) Whisk the egg whites until stiff then add the sugar a tablespoon at a time; continue whisking until very stiff. Whisk in the vinegar and vanilla essence.

3) Fold in the nuts. Divide the mixture between the two tins and smooth down. Bake for 30–40 minutes at 190°C (375°F) Gas Mark 5. Cool on a rack then peel off the paper.

4) Whisk the cream until stiff.

5) Put the bottom meringue onto a serving plate and pile some cream on top, reserving the rest to pipe rosettes onto the top layer. Put all but about 6 (according to the number of cream rosettes) of the raspberries on top of the cream followed by the meringue top. Pipe rosette decorations with the reserved cream and leave in a cool place until needed.

To Serve

Pop a raspberry on top of each cream rosette and dust the top of the cake with icing sugar. The cake should cut without splintering but still be crispy.

N.B. Because the meringue is brittle this dessert is best finished a couple of hours before it's needed.

Timetables

These timetables are worked out to give a 1.0 p.m. sitting-down time.

TIMETABLE FOR MENU 18

Homemade Creamy Mushroom Soup

. . .

Roast Ribs of Beef, Yorkshire Puddings,
Horseradish Sauce, Roast Potatoes,
Parsnips and Onions, Crunchy White
Cabbage, Carrots, Gravy

. . .

Apple Pie and Cheese

The Day Before
Make pastry.

Early in the Morning
Make up apple pie and refrigerate.
Sauté mushrooms and cook soup. Set aside.
Prepare vegetables and horseradish.
Mix Yorkshire pudding and refrigerate.
Par-boil potatoes, parsnips and onions.

Start Time .... a.m.
Place meat in oven.

To Finish Cooking
12.00 noon   Heat dripping and put potatoes, parsnips and onions into oven.

12.30 p.m.   Put apple pie into oven.

12.40 p.m.   Take meat out of oven and set aside to keep warm. Turn up the heat, put Yorkshire puddings at top of oven, put apple pie on lower shelf. Put on carrots to cook. Put plates to warm. Start to make gravy.

12.50 p.m.   Put soup on to warm through.

12.55 p.m.   Cook cabbage for 5 minutes, drain, cover, set aside to keep warm.

 1.00 p.m.   Serve soup. Check apple pie.
              Carve and serve the roast beef.
              Take the Yorkshire puddings from the oven at the very last minute.

TIMETABLE FOR MENU NO. 19

Carrot and Coriander Soup
· · ·
Roast Leg of Pork, Sage and Onion Balls, Apple Sauce, Brussels Sprouts, Glazed Carrots, Creamed Potatoes, Roast Potatoes
· · ·
Light Syrup Pudding

The Day Before
Make soup   } if already made and
Make apple sauce   } frozen, take out of the
Make sage and onion balls. } freezer.

Early in the Morning
Prepare vegetables.
Par-boil potatoes for roasting.
Make up pudding, put on to cook at 11.15 a.m.

Start Time .... a.m.
Put pork in oven.

To Finish Cooking

12.00 noon Heat dripping and put potatoes for roasting into oven.
Put carrots into oven.

12.15 p.m. Put sage and onion balls into oven.

12.30 p.m. Put potatoes for mashing on to simmer.
Start custard (if making).

12.40 p.m. Take meat out of oven, and set aside to keep warm. Put plates to warm.
Put soup to warm through gently.
Start making gravy.

12.50 p.m. Put on sprouts to cook. Take pudding from heat.

1.00 p.m. Drain the sprouts, mash the potatoes; set aside to keep warm. Serve the soup, checking the gravy and the custard before sitting down yourself.

TIMETABLE FOR MENU NO. 20

Small Mushroom Tartlets
· · ·
Whole Poached Salmon, Hollandaise Sauce, Jersey Potatoes, Fresh Asparagus
· · ·
Hazelnut Meringue with Raspberries

The Day Before

Make court bouillon.
Make pastry.
Make meringues.
Clean salmon.

Early in the Morning

Roll out pastry and line patty tins.
Scrub potatoes (don't peel).
Trim asparagus.
Whip up cream and assemble meringue.

Start Time .... a.m.

To Finish Cooking

12.30 p.m.   Put salmon on to cook.

12.40 p.m.   Put pastry in oven to cook.
             Start to prepare mushrooms and sauce.

12.45 p.m.   Put potatoes on to cook.
             Put asparagus on to cook.
             Start hollandaise sauce.

12.50 p.m.   Check potatoes and asparagus. When ready,
             drain and set aside to keep warm.

12.55 p.m.   Check pastry, finish mushrooms and sauce.
             Finish hollandaise and set aside to keep
             warm.

 1.00 p.m.   Put raspberry decoration on top of meringue.
             Fill and serve mushroom tarts.

Basic Preparations

WHITE SAUCE (base for cheese or parsley sauces)

There are two easy ways to make the basic sauce, the all-in-one method and the more classic roux method. The choice is yours but if the liquid to be added is warm, as in the fish pie recipe for instance, then the roux method must be used.

All-In-One Method
    25g (1 oz) butter
    25g (1 oz) flour
    300ml (½ pint) milk
    salt

To Cook
    Put all the ingredients into a pan *cold* and heat through, gently whisking all the time. When the sauce comes to the boil simmer for 2–3 minutes. Flavour as required (see note at end of recipe).

Roux Method
    25g (1 oz) butter
    25g (1 oz) flour
    300ml (½ pint) milk
    salt

To Cook
1) Melt the butter in a small pan. Add the flour and a pinch of salt and stir over a gentle heat for 2 minutes; do not allow to brown. Remove from the heat.
2) Slowly whisk in the milk, return to the heat and bring

to the boil stirring all the time; simmer gently for 2 minutes. Flavour as required (see note below).

N.B. To make cheese sauce add 50g (2 oz) of grated cheese after simmering. To make parsley sauce add 2–3 tablespoons freshly chopped parsley after simmering.

LIGHT VINAIGRETTE

1 tablespoon red or white wine vinegar *or* lemon juice or both mixed
salt and freshly ground black pepper
3 tablespoons olive oil

To Make
Beat the salt and a few grindings of pepper in the vinegar until dissolved. Beat in the olive oil a spoonful at a time.

SLOE GIN (Make 3—4 weeks before Christmas)

800g (1 lb) sloe berries
800g (1 lb) caster sugar
1 gin bottle with screw cap and enough gin to cover the fruit and sugar

To Make
1) Put the berries and sugar into the bottle. Top up with gin.
2) Screw up tightly and invert once or twice to mix.
3) Invert once or twice each week to blend contents.
4) Strain and drink whenever you need something really warming!

SHORTCRUST PASTRY

200g (8 oz) plain flour
pinch of salt
50g (2 oz) lard
50g (2 oz) margarine
cold water to mix

To Make
1) Sift the flour and salt together in a large mixing bowl.
2) Cut the lard and margarine into small pieces, add the flour mixture and rub in with fingertips until the mixture resembles breadcrumbs.
3) Add 3–4 tablespoons of cold water and stir with a fork, adding a little more water if necessary to bind the mixture together.
4) Knead lightly and allow to rest for 30 minutes.

CHRISTMAS CAKE

To give a 20cm (8in) diameter cake
400g (1 lb) sultanas
300g (12 oz) raisins
200g (8 oz) glacé cherries
100g (4 oz) candied peel
100g (4 oz) chopped almonds
200g (8 oz) plain flour
pinch of salt
1 teaspoon nutmeg and mace mixed together
150g (6 oz) butter
150g (6 oz) soft brown sugar
4 eggs
3 tablespoons brandy
1 teaspoon lemon juice

To Cook

1) Line a 20cm (8in) cake tin with a double layer of greaseproof paper.
2) Mix the fruit and almonds together in a large bowl.
3) Sieve the flour, add the salt, nutmeg and mace, mix well and add about a third of this mixture to the fruit.
4) Cream the butter, add the sugar and beat until thick and creamy. Beat in the eggs one at a time, then fold in half the remaining flour.
5) Fold in the fruit mixture, then the remaining flour and finally the brandy and lemon juice.
6) Turn the mixture into the cake tin, smooth the surface with a sprinkling of water and bake at 180°C (350°F) Gas Mark 4 for about 1 hour. Reduce the heat to 160°C (325°F) Gas Mark 3 and bake for a further 1 hour. Pierce with a skewer to test whether the inside is cooked through. (If the skewer comes away clean the cake is cooked.)
7) Allow the cake to cool in the tin then turn out onto a wire rack. When completely cool wrap in foil and store until needed. One week before Christmas cover with almond paste, and ice to taste.

ALMOND PASTE

200g (8 oz) ground almonds
150g (6 oz) caster sugar
100g (4 oz) icing sugar
1 egg
2 tablespoons lemon juice
3–4 drops vanilla essence

To Make

1) Mix the almonds with the sugars. Beat the egg with the lemon juice and vanilla essence and add to the almonds.

2) Knead well to a smooth paste adding a little more lemon juice if needed.

APRICOT GLAZE

6 tablespoons apricot jam
2 tablespoons water

To Make
Put the jam and water into a pan, heat until the jam dissolves, simmer for 2–3 minutes. Strain.

ICING

4 egg whites
800g (2 lb) icing sugar
1 tablespoon lemon juice
2 teaspoons glycerine

To Make
1) Whisk the egg whites until frothy. Stir in the sugar a spoonful at a time, adding the lemon juice about halfway through. Beat well.
2) Stir in the glycerine and allow to stand, covered, overnight before using.

To Finish the Cake
1) If liked, prick the surface of the cake and pour over some brandy; allow to soak in well.
2) Brush the cake with apricot glaze; this helps the almond paste adhere to the cake.
3) Using your hands, flatten the almond paste and mould

to the cake in two pieces, one for the top and one for the sides. Use a rolling pin very lightly to smooth out.

4) Allow to stand for two days then ice as preferred.

To Serve

A wedge of good sharp cheese, Wensleydale, Cheshire or Lancashire, is the traditional northern accompaniment for Christmas Cake.

Index